ISLAM TAUGHT ME

A Spiritual Guide to Deepening Your Faith and Your Relationship with Allah سبحانه وتعالى

NAIMA ABDULLAH

ISLAM TAUGHT ME

Edited by:
Amel S. Abdullah

Cover by:
Yasser Elgazzar

بسم الله الرحمن الرحيم

IN THE NAME OF ALLAH

Table Of Contents

Introduction

"Allāh is the Light of the heavens and the earth. The example of His light is like a niche within which is a lamp, the lamp is within glass, the glass as if it were a pearly [white] star lit from [the oil of] a blessed olive tree, neither of the east nor of the west, whose oil would almost glow even if untouched by fire. Light upon light. Allāh guides to His light whom He wills. And Allāh presents examples for the people, and Allāh is Knowing of all things."

— Sūrat al-Nūr (Qurʾān 24:35)

While those who are practicing Islam perform certain rituals required of a believer, such as praying five times a day and fasting during the holy month of Ramaḍān, how many understand the real meaning of these rituals and discover their true purpose as Allāh ﷻ wants for us? How many of us actually feel the glow of Allāh's light in our lives?

Allāh ﷻ has gifted us with the immense blessing and miracle of the Qurʾān, but have we only learned to recite the Qurʾān and memorize some of its verses to meet the requirements of Islamic prayer, or have we allowed the Qurʾān to become a vital part of our lives so that we may become enlightened and taste the sweetness of faith?

These and other thoughts are what motivated me to write this inspirational Islamic book—because I wanted to share some of the unique spiritual gems found in Islam with people from around the world. Whether you are already a Muslim or are only beginning to explore Islam, I hope you will gain new insights into this faith that you were not previously aware of.

Yet the book does not only contain quotes from the Qurʾān. You will also find numerous quotes from the sayings of Prophet Muḥammad ﷺ, his noble Companions (may Allāh ﷻ be pleased with them all), and early Muslim scholars.

The quotes chosen for inclusion in this book are mainly focused on a few key themes, such as improving one's relationship with the Creator and cultivating the traits of a believer. Each quote is accompanied by a short passage that is intended to soothe the heart with comforting words that help one deal with life's most difficult challenges in a positive Islamic manner that is both practical and uplifting.

After thanking Allāh ﷻ for making it possible for me to write this book, I would also like to thank the publisher **(Br. Mouad Garwan)** for providing me with the opportunity to write it.

Beyond that, I would also like to express my deepest gratitude to my beloved parents for the positive role they have played in my life as well as in this book (may Allāh bless them both). Among other things, my mother edited the book and gave me valuable feedback about the structure and content of the passages, while my father has long inspired me to enhance my knowledge of the Qurʾān and Islam.

I dedicate this book to both of my parents, to my four siblings, to every Muslim and Muslimah, and to anyone who is interested in discovering the noble teachings of Islam. May Allāh ﷻ bless and guide us all.

Finally, I pray to Allāh that this book has a positive impact on whoever reads it, that it brings him or her closer to the essence of Islam, and that Allāh ﷻ accepts it as a good deed. ***Āmīn***.

— Naima Abdullah

FOLLOW ALLĀH'S GUIDANCE

"...And when guidance comes to you from Me, whoever follows My guidance - there will be no fear concerning them, nor will they grieve."

— *Sūrat al-Baqarah (Qur'ān 2:38)*

This is a promise from Allāh ﷻ that whosoever follows His guidance shall never be sad or afraid.

Have you ever come across a believing Muslim who always seems to be in a state of contentment no matter what hardships he or she may be going through?

Well, this is his secret.

He is following Allāh's guidance.

But what is Allāh's guidance? And how do we follow it?

Ever since the creation of the first human being on Earth, the Ever-Merciful Allāh has been sending His guidance to humankind so that we may follow the right path—and this is how it shall be until the end of time.

Allāh ﷻ tells us in *Sūrat al-Naml:*

> And say, "All praise is due to Allāh. He will show you His signs, and you will recognize them. And your Lord is not unaware of what you do."
> *(Qur'ān 27: 93)*

So, open your mind, and open your heart.

Read the Qur'ān, understand the Qur'ān, and most importantly: Act upon the Qur'ān.

In addition: Always ask Allāh for His guidance.

Without a doubt, you will soon find that it has been granted to you, and you will definitely see clear evidence of this when a sense of contentment washes over your heart.

And remember, dear believer...

Any worldly success achieved in this life is fleeting and will not be blessed if one does not stay away from the things that Allāh ﷻ has forbidden to us. Understanding this is an important part of contentment that will also lead to contentment in the Hereafter, *in shā' Allāh.*

But does finding contentment with Allāh's decree mean that a true believer will never experience sadness in his or her life?

Let us explore this topic in the pages that follow.

Do Not Grieve

"And the pains of childbirth drove her to the trunk of a palm tree. She said, 'Oh, I wish I had died before this and was in oblivion, forgotten.' But he called her from below her, 'Do not grieve; your Lord has provided beneath you a stream.'"

— *Sūrat Maryam (Qur'ān 19:23–24)*

The above verses come from the story of Maryam bt. ʿImrān, the pious mother of Prophet ʿĪsá (Jesus) (PBUH).

Maryam (AS) was known among her people for her great piety—and Allāh ﷻ honored her by granting her a very special status that no woman had ever been granted before, choosing her "above the women of the worlds," as described in *Sūrat Āli ʿImrān (Qur'ān 3:42).*

Her whole life was dedicated to worshiping Allāh ﷻ and pleasing Him.

She was a true believer and content with Allāh's decree.

Yet she went through severe distress.

Although she had never been married or touched by any man (and remained chaste throughout her life), it was Allāh's will for her to give birth to a child.

When that moment finally arrived, she experienced so much pain (both mentally and physically) that she wished she had been dead and forgotten long ago.

But it was precisely at that very dark point in time that Allāh ﷻ showered Maryam (AS) with His infinite mercy...all because she was a true believer.

O Maryam, do not grieve! Allāh is with you and taking care of you. Open your eyes to see the blessings Allāh is providing you with! You are not alone!

This was the message conveyed to Maryam (AS) in the above verses.

And so it is with the true believer.

Whenever you are sad, desperate, or feeling down, take a deep breath, and look around you. Allāh ﷻ is with you, and He will never leave you alone!

His gentleness can be spotted in somebody's help, smile, or even a drink of water...

O believer, do not grieve...

Trust in Allāh

"And the heart of Mūsá's mother became empty [of all else]. She was about to disclose [the matter concerning] him had We not bound fast her heart that she would be of the believers."

— *Sūrat al-Qaṣaṣ (Qurʾān 28:10)*

The mother of Prophet Mūsá (Moses) (PBUH) was another believing woman who experienced overwhelming fear and sadness during a difficult situation.

Since the oldest of times, there had been evil people practicing oppression in different ways; here in the story of Mūsá (PBUH), it was Firʿawn, an arrogant pharaoh who was so enamored with his own power that he feared one day losing it to someone else. In his mind, every newborn boy posed a threat to his rule, so he slaughtered every one of them and only allowed the females to live.

When Mūsá's mother gave birth to him, Allāh ﷻ inspired her to "cast him into the river" and told her not to fear or grieve. "We will return him to you," Allāh promised her.

Yet when the moment came, it was difficult and frightening.

Mūsá's mother was a mother, after all.

But because she had faith, because she trusted Allāh, Allāh bound fast her heart.

If patience was easy, it would not be called patience, yet it is a blessing from Allāh provided to the righteous.

In the verses that complete the story, we find that Allāh ﷻ indeed fulfilled His promise to Mūsá's mother, easing the path for Mūsá (PBUH) to be saved, nurtured, and ultimately returned back to his mother.

Trust in Allāh ﷻ, and He will comfort you no matter how complex the situation may seem...

No matter how hard the decisions were that you had to make...

And no matter what type of oppression you were living under.

I am sure, dear reader, that you have experienced this many times in your own life, in different situations.

Because you had faith, and because you were patient and trusted in Allāh, He took away your fear and sadness and filled your heart with contentment.

It is this blissful state of contentment that allows one to taste the sweetness of faith...when everything you say or do in life is purely for the sake of Allāh, and you fully believe that He loves you and is taking care of you during even the hardest of times.

But what can you do to achieve this level of faith? Let us find out what Prophet Muḥammad ﷺ had to say about this very topic.

Discover the Sweetness of Faith

"Whosoever possesses three traits within himself will taste the sweetness of faith: One who loves Allāh and His Messenger more than anything else; one who loves another person solely for the sake of Allāh; and one who hates to return to kufr (disbelief), just as he hates to be thrown into the Fire."

— A saying of Prophet Muḥammad ﷺ (Ṣaḥīḥ al-Bukhārī, No. 16)

This is the bottom line.

To find the sweetness of faith, you first have to love Allāh more than anyone, more than anything. And even when you love someone, it has to be solely for the sake of Allāh.

Anyone can claim to love Allāh, but as we all know, there is a big difference between saying you love someone and actually acting upon that love.

So, how do we show our love to Allāh?

By following Allāh's guidance, which means that we need to understand the teachings of our faith and act upon them, even when we are presented with difficult or unpleasant choices that require us to make sacrifices for His sake.

Maybe you have faced such dilemmas in your own life...like deciding not to attend your best friend's wedding because you knew that some activities there would be displeasing to Allāh...or choosing not to wear make-up to school or work because you knew that a Muslim must remain modest outside of the home. You stayed honest, even when lying was easier—and you stayed chaste, even when it felt like everyone around you was in a relationship.

Such choices are not always easy, and do not always represent what the society around us favors.

But when you love Allāh more than anything else, it becomes much easier to show your love in practical terms. And once this becomes your way of life, your heart will become much calmer; it will even dislike what Allāh has prohibited on its own.

Ask Allāh to help you, to make it easy for you.

Remember that our time in this world is short, and it won't be long before we meet Allāh ﷻ in the Hereafter, so let us take every opportunity to please Him before that day comes.

Aim to be among the people whom the angels greet at the gates of Paradise with the following words:

> "Peace be upon you for what you patiently endured. And excellent is the final abode."
> — *Sūrat al-Ra'd (Qur'ān 13:24)*

Strive for Balance

"In this world, women and perfume have been made dear to me, and my comfort has been provided in prayer."

— A saying of Prophet Muḥammad ﷺ (Sunan al-Nasā'ī, No. 3939)

In this ḥadīth, Prophet Muḥammad ﷺ is teaching us a very important lesson.

Enjoy the blessings that Allāh ﷻ has provided you with in this worldly life.

It may be that you like art, fashion, traveling, or trying new kinds of food among your other interests.

Very well, enjoy every single one of them. Cultivating your interests is actually a means of thanking Allāh for the blessings of this life (and for the blessing of life itself).

Dress neatly, and apply perfume. Be kind to your spouse, and show love to him or her.

The Prophet ﷺ himself expressed that his wives were among those dearest to him in this life, yet it was prayer that gave him comfort.

Enjoy your worldly life while pleasing Allāh and following His guidance.

Love your spouse, but for the sake of Allāh.

Enjoy your money, but also give to the poor.

Study, work, and socialize, but remember to love Allāh more than all that.

Pray, fast, and read the Qur'ān, but don't play the role of a monk. There is no such thing in Islam.

Islam is meant to help us achieve balance in life.

By following its noble teachings, we become people of faith who gain the tools necessary for building a better society.

> "But seek, through that which Allāh has given you, the abode of the Hereafter; and [yet], do not forget your share of the world. And do good as Allāh has done good to you. And desire not corruption in the land. Indeed, Allāh does not like corrupters."
> — *Sūrat al-Qaṣaṣ (Qur'ān 28:77)*

Protect Your Heart

"True happiness is that of the Hereafter."

— Abū Ḥāmid al-Ghazālī (d. 1111)

To live a happy life in the Hereafter, we must live in this worldly life with the aim of pleasing Allāh with every step we take.

Do not become so enamored by this worldly life that you start to neglect, or even forget, your beliefs and principles. This is not what Allāh ﷻ wants for us as believers.

This often happens gradually, when a person starts to convince him or herself that various things are okay to do (even though they aren't), starting with things that may seem trivial or unimportant at first.

Allāh won't punish me for that; I'm a good person! So what if I went to a friend's party even though the guests were smoking, drinking, and freely socializing with the opposite gender? I'm not doing the ḥarām stuff; I'm just having fun! So what if I use a few curse words here and there? It doesn't make me a bad person! So what if I take off my ḥijāb? I'm still a believer! So what if I'm not truthful in my dealings with people? Allāh knows that my heart is pure!

Do you see the problem here?

The thing is, my dear Muslim, that you can't actually separate your practice of Islam from the things you say and do; it is impossible.

Prophet Muḥammad ﷺ told us:

> "There is no heart that is not between two of the Fingers of the Most Merciful. If He wills, He guides it and if He wills, He sends it astray."
> *(Sunan Ibn Mājah, No. 199)*

The inclinations of a heart may change, so protect your heart by realizing that your heart is inextricably connected to your actions and to your speech, just as your actions and your speech are inextricably connected to your heart.

Then make the same supplication taught to us by the Prophet ﷺ:

> "O You Who makes hearts steadfast, make our hearts steadfast in adhering to Your religion."
> *(Sunan Ibn Mājah, No. 199)*

Remaining steadfast is how a person may achieve true happiness in both this life and in the Hereafter.

Read the Qur'ān

"And We send down of the Qur'ān that which is healing and mercy for the believers..."

— Sūrat al-Isrā' (Qur'ān 17:82)

O true believer, if you are looking for something to cure your heart from ailments such as heartbreak, sadness, and sorrow...

And if you wish to protect it from becoming cold, hard, and lifeless...

Do not go looking too far away, for it is right next to you; you just need to open it.

I am speaking of the Qur'ān, the words of the Almighty Allāh, Who told us in a verse from *Sūrat al-Baqarah:*

> "...I am the Accepting of Repentance, the Merciful."
> *(Qur'ān 2:160)*

In the Qur'ān, Allāh ﷻ is speaking directly to you and me both; in fact, He is speaking to all of humanity. Within its pages, we find stories of the prophets and the righteous alongside stories of the wrongdoers.

Allāh teaches us in the Qur'ān how to have good morals, how to worship Him correctly, and how to be kind and patient. He warns us not to be among those who lose the blessings of both the worldly life and the Hereafter, and even tells us directly how to obtain the reward of Paradise as our final abode.

What greater mercy and healing could one ever seek?

Allāh, the One Who created you, is speaking to you directly through His Holy Book that He promised to preserve until the end of time.

So, what are you waiting for? Pick up your Qurʾān, and start reading it today!

Don't Let Your Sins Defeat You

"My sin burdened me heavily. But when I measured it against Your Grace, O Lord, Your forgiveness came out greater."

— Imām al-Shāfiʿī (d. 820)

Never think that your sins are greater than Allāh's mercy.

As good Muslims, we try our best not to engage in sinful acts.

But we are the children of Ādam, and we know from a saying of Prophet Muḥammad ﷺ that:

> "All the sons of Ādam are sinners, but the best of sinners are those who repent often."
> *(Sunan Ibn Mājah, No. 4251)*

Allāh ﷻ emphasized this in many verses of the Qurʾān, including this one from *Sūrat al-Nisāʾ*:

> "And whoever does a wrong or wrongs himself but then seeks the forgiveness of Allāh will find Allāh Forgiving and Merciful."
> *(Qurʾān 4:110)*

A sin should never be something that brings your spiritual progress to a halt or prevents you from doing good deeds.

The most important thing is that you repent and never do it again.

Oh, but what if you did?

Then you must try again to refrain from that sin. Do not feel despair; rather keep asking Allāh to forgive you and help you stop whatever sin you are doing.

And remember: Allāh is the Most Forgiving and the Most Merciful. You just have to be sincere in your repentance.

Be Gentle

"Verily, Allāh is gentle, and He loves gentleness. He rewards for gentleness what is not granted for harshness, and He does not reward anything else like it."

— A saying of Prophet Muḥammad ﷺ (Ṣaḥīḥ Muslim, No. 2593)

Some mistakenly think that showing gentleness or kindness to others is a form of weakness. In reality, however, it is a point of strength that Allāh ﷻ has blessed some of us with. Self-control is not always easy, so a person who possesses the ability to be gentle with others despite his own difficulties in life is truly blessed and loved by Allāh, He Who is gentle and Who loves gentleness.

Being gentle does not mean allowing others to take advantage of you; rather, it means to be respectful, easygoing, and empathetic, all for Allāh's sake.

Likewise, being gentle does not mean that you should not stand up for your rights, but one should always do so in a fair and respectful manner.

Prophet Muḥammad ﷺ was known for being a very gentle person, yet he was a great leader who changed the entire course of history, and gentleness was actually the very reason why he succeeded!

As Allāh ﷻ tells us in a verse from *Sūrat Āli 'Imrān:*

> "So by mercy from Allāh, [O Muḥammad], you were lenient with them. And if you had been rude [in speech] and harsh in heart, they would have disbanded from about you."
> *(Qur'ān 3:159)*

If you are preaching Islam with the intention of pleasing Allāh and enlightening others, then you should be gentle with those you are trying to reach.

If you wish to be a successful parent, then be gentle with your spouse as well as with your children. Show them love and patience as you strive to understand them.

Be gentle with your mother and father; smile with them, and do what you can to make them happy. Be gentle with your siblings, with your friends, and with strangers. Be gentle with plants and animals, too...

Aren't they also part of Allāh's vast creation?

Even if you had to slaughter an animal (for food), the Prophet ﷺ told us that a person should "sharpen his knife and give ease to his animal (in order to reduce his pain)." *(Riyāḍ al-Ṣāliḥīn, No. 639)*

O you who always strives to be kind and gentle, congratulations to you! The Almighty Allāh is pleased with you and will grant you a special reward unlike any other reward from Him.

CHERISH YOUR DAUGHTERS

"I have not seen anyone more closely resemble the disposition, mannerisms, and characteristics of the Messenger of Allāh ﷺ than his daughter Fāṭimah, may Allāh honor her countenance. If she entered his home, the Prophet would stand for her, take her by the hand, kiss her, and seat her in his place. If the Prophet entered her home, she would stand for him, take him by the hand, kiss him, and seat him in her place."

— ʿĀʾishah (RA) (Sunan Abī Dāʾūd, No. 5217)

This quote demonstrates the beautiful relationship between a father and his daughter.

Fāṭimah al-Zahrāʾ (RA) was the youngest daughter of Prophet Muḥammad ﷺ, and she was very special to him. He once said:

> "Verily, she is but a part of me. I am upset by what upsets her, and I am harmed by what harms her."
> *(Ṣaḥīḥ al-Bukhārī, No. 4932)*

There is nothing greater than a daughter's love, and Prophet Muḥammad ﷺ described daughters as "your precious companions." *(Musnad Aḥmad, No. 16922)*

Love them, cherish them, be kind to them, support them, and do not be harsh with them.

If you have a daughter, you are truly blessed by Allāh ﷻ.

Prophet Muḥammad ﷺ said:

> "He who has a daughter and does not bury her alive, or humiliate her, or prefer his sons over her, will enter Paradise due to her."
> *(Sunan Abī Dā'ūd, No. 5146)*

He also said:

> "If someone has three daughters and is patient with them, gives them food and drink, and clothes them, then they will be his shield from the Hellfire on the Day of Resurrection."
> *(Sunan Ibn Mājah, No. 3669)*

Be Good to Women

"The best of you are the best to their women."

— A saying of Prophet Muḥammad ﷺ (Sunan Ibn Mājah, No. 1978)

Just as one must be good to his daughters, Prophet Muḥammad ﷺ also told his Companions that the best of men is he who is best to his women.

Such a man shows love, respect, and gentleness to all of his female relatives, including his mother, his wife, his aunts, his sisters, and his daughters.

So, smile with the women in your life, and make them happy. Share ideas with them, consult with them, hug them, and bring them gifts.

Islam teaches us that love, respect, and affection for one's female relatives is what helps makes a man a man—the best of all men.

The best to Allāh.

Support Your Husband

Jibrīl (Gabriel) (AS) came to the Prophet ﷺ and said, "O Messenger of Allāh! Khadījah is coming to you with a dish [of food or soup]. When she reaches you, greet her on behalf of her Lord [Allāh] and on my behalf, and give her the glad tidings of a palace of qaṣab [hollowed pearls] in Paradise wherein there will be neither any disturbance nor any fatigue."

— *Ṣaḥīḥ al-Bukhārī, No. 3820*

Khadījah bt. Khuwaylid (RA) was a righteous noblewoman and the beloved first wife of Prophet Muḥammad ﷺ.

She believed in the Prophet ﷺ and stood with him during the toughest of times.

She was a great wife; that's why Allāh ﷻ promised her a great reward and honored her by telling the Prophet ﷺ to greet her on behalf of her Lord.

My dear sister in Islam...

To have a healthy and blessed married life, support your husband, and show him love, respect, patience, and understanding.

Just as you want him to care for you, you should also care for him in the same manner.

Work with him to get through any hardships, and always let Islamic morals be the foundation of your sacred relationship.

Be a righteous noblewoman like Khadījah (RA)...

And may Allāh be pleased with you and grant you Jannah.

Be Proud of Your Spouse

"...She believed in me when no one else did; she accepted Islam when people rejected me; and she helped and comforted me when there was no one else to lend me a helping hand..."

— A saying of Prophet Muḥammad ﷺ (Ṣaḥīḥ al-Bukhārī, No. 3821)

This narration about the Prophet's beloved first wife, Khadījah (RA), again illustrates the importance of supporting one's spouse during life's trials. But another important lesson can also be found within these beautiful, heartfelt words, which is that one should also be proud of his or her spouse.

Be proud of your spouse, and do not ever feel embarrassed or ashamed to acknowledge his or her positive qualities and virtues.

One should also never forget this blessed relationship in the future if it happened that your spouse passed away before you did and you ended up marrying another person. In fact, the Prophet ﷺ said the above words when recalling Khadījah's many virtues after her death.

Always pray for your deceased spouse, give charity on their behalf, and be good to their family and friends just like Prophet Muḥammad ﷺ was good to Khadījah's relatives after she passed away.

My dear sister in Islam, be a good wife who appreciates her husband, as this is something your husband will always appreciate and remember.

Likewise to my brother in Islam: Be a good, loving husband who is always grateful and thankful for the great blessing of a good wife.

May Allāh ﷻ bless both of you in your marriages and beyond.

Give Freely

"Generosity and openhandedness cover your flaws in both the Dunyā and the Ākhirah."

— Imām al-Shāfi'ī

Do you feel like you have a lot of shortcomings?

Then, give.

Give to the poor and to the needy. Give to your siblings, to your spouse, to your children, and to your parents.

Give with a sincere heart, with the pure intention of pleasing Allāh and bringing happiness to the people you give to.

As Allāh ﷻ tells us in the verses of *Sūrat al-Layl:*

> "As for he who gives and fears Allāh and believes in the best [reward], We will ease him toward ease."
> *(Qur'ān 92:5–7)*

You will gain five things:

- The pleasure of alleviating another person's suffering;
- The alleviation of your own suffering;
- Concealment of your flaws in this worldly life (the Dunyā);
- Concealment of your flaws in the Hereafter (the Ākhirah);
- The happiness that comes with Allāh being pleased with you.

Keep Righteous Company

"The company of the righteous transforms six things within a person, replacing doubt with certainty; pretension with sincerity; forgetfulness of Allāh with the remembrance of Allāh; a desire for worldly life with a desire for the Hereafter; arrogance with humbleness; and negative objectives with [those that are positive]."

— Ibn al-Qayyim (d. 1350)

Surrounding ourselves with righteous friends is very important for the soul.

We often subconsciously adopt the traits of our friends, as we engage in a lot of activities together.

When assessing your friendships, always ask yourself whether the company of a particular person has been a positive or a negative influence on your thoughts and behaviors.

Things to think about include the following:

- Have I become more materialistic as the result of this friendship? Or have I become humbler?
- Am I okay with hearing (and using) bad language, or has my heart moved away from it?
- Have I started to miss prayers? Or do my friends and I always try to remind each other when it is time to pray?

It is good to evaluate the impact of your friendships on you every now and then, making changes as needed.

Also remember the words of Prophet Muḥammad ﷺ, who said:

"The example of a good companion in comparison with a bad one is like that of the musk seller and the blacksmith's bellows (or furnace); from the first, you would either buy musk or enjoy its pleasant fragrance, while the bellows would either burn your flesh or your clothing, or you would [be faced with] the bad odor."
(Ṣaḥīḥ al-Bukhārī, No. 2101)

Seek Allāh's Pardon

"The heart becoming rusty is due to two matters: sins and neglecting the remembrance of Allāh. Likewise, it is cleansed and polished by two things: istighfār and dhikr."

— *Ibn al-Qayyim*

Make *istighfār* (seeking pardon from Allāh) and *dhikr* (remembrance of Allāh) a daily habit...something you do at least twice a day—once when you wake up, and once before you go to sleep.

Istighfār and *dhikr* are among the things that keep your heart fully intact. Regularly seeking Allāh's pardon may also increase a person's blessings and *rizq* (sustenance).

As Prophet Muḥammad ﷺ informed us:

> "If anyone constantly seeks pardon (from Allāh), Allāh will appoint for him a way out of every distress, and a relief from every anxiety, and He will provide sustenance for him from where he does not expect it."
> *(Riyāḍ al-Ṣāliḥīn, No. 1873)*

Be Humble and Glorify Allāh

"And had he not been of those who exalt Allāh he would have remained inside its belly until the Day they are resurrected."

— *Sūrat al-Ṣāffāt (Qur'ān 37:143–144)*

The story of Prophet Yūnus (Jonah) (PBUH) tells us that disobeying Allāh or not having enough patience may lead to bad consequences.

Yet if you were a true believer and repented to Allāh, He shall save you, as shown in the verses of *Sūrat al-Anbiyā' (Qur'ān 21:87–88)*, where more of this story can be found.

Prophet Yūnus (PBUH) was swallowed by a fish after he had "given up hope on his people prematurely and left them without permission from Allāh." [1]

In that moment of despair, he called out to Allāh:

> "There is no deity except You; exalted are You. Indeed, I have been of the wrongdoers."
> *(Qur'ān 21:87)*

Allāh says that if Yūnus (PBUH) hadn't been among those who glorify Allāh, he would not have been saved.

But because he was sincere, Allāh accepted his repentance and saved him.

When you are in a state of darkness due to something wrong you did, do NOT despair of Allāh's mercy.

1. https://quranenc.com/ar/browse/english_saheeh/37 (see explanation under Qur'ān 37:142).

The only thing that will save you is your repentance to Allāh.

Distancing yourself from Allāh will never help you.

So, humble yourself, and ask Allāh for forgiveness and help.

He will definitely save you just as he saved Yūnus (PBUH), and just as He always saves the believers!

Strive for Happiness in the Hereafter

"[Some] faces, that Day, will be radiant, looking at their Lord."

— Sūrat al-Qiyāmah (Qur'ān 75:22–23)

Aim to be of the people whose faces are full of light and happiness in the Hereafter.

These are the blessed individuals who will have the privilege of gazing at Allāh's exalted face, which has no equal.

But who, exactly, are these blessed individuals?

The believers! The ones who prayed, fasted, and gave charity...

Those who were truthful, kind, and fair to others...

Those who loved Allāh ﷻ more than anything in this entire universe.

They will see their Lord, and they will be blessed with a happiness of the type that never diminishes or fades.

Look for the Good in People

"O you who have believed, avoid suspicion as much (as possible). Indeed, some suspicion is a sin."

— *Sūrat al-Ḥujurāt (Qur'ān 49:12)*

This verse of the Qur'ān is related to *ḥusn al-ẓann* (assuming the best of others).

It's the thing that spreads love and the spirit of brotherhood and sisterhood in society.

In your everyday life, you may encounter people who seem unfriendly even though they aren't truly like that. Like many, it may just be that they put on a mask of sternness as a survival mechanism.

You might be tempted to deal with such people in the same manner (leading to enmity between you). Another option is to have patience as you try to bring out the best in them.

If you have ever tried both ways, you probably noticed a big difference in the outcomes you got.

When you assume the worst of someone, that person will often display a negative attitude and prove your assumptions correct. But if you put some effort into finding the same person's good side, then everything changes!

Think of teachers who work hard to reach their difficult students. It's the same type of challenge.

Yes, bad people exist, and people do have negative traits.

Some people are actually evil, and one must be aware of this.

One should not ever tolerate evil or be deceived by it.

If you're dealing with the average person, however, it is different. Most people are decent.

So, keep your eyes open for a person's positive qualities, and try to connect with them based on positive assumptions rather than on ones that are negative.

You may be the reason for someone to take off the mask they've been wearing for a long time.

You may be the reason for someone to see goodness in others again!

That is how you spread goodness in society.

As Allāh ﷻ tells us in a verse from *Sūrat al-Raʿd:*

> "Indeed, Allāh will not change the condition of a people until they change what is in themselves."
> *(Qur'ān 13:11)*

ALLOW OTHERS TO HELP

"And appoint for me a minister [i.e., assistant] from my family: Hārūn, my brother. Increase through him my strength, and let him share my task."

— *Sūrat Ṭā-Hā (Qur'ān 20:29–32)*

It is okay to ask your fellow man for help; you actually should.

Allāh ﷻ created us with varied abilities.

Knowing when to delegate tasks to others and benefit from their assistance is a major strength and not a weakness as some may believe.

It means that you know how to cooperate, and that you are humble enough to accept other ways of doing things. When everybody puts their efforts into doing the things they are most qualified to do, this results in better outcomes as well.

Obtaining the help of others when needed is a blessing from Allāh to ease our journey in life.

Do not carry all the burden by yourself! Look around, and you will find dozens of helping hands waiting to assist you...trustworthy people who are delighted to share their skills, knowledge, and experience for the sake of Allāh.

So, trust in people, and allow them to shine...

Just like Prophet Mūsá (Moses) (PBUH) had trust in his brother Hārūn (Aaron) (PBUH) and asked Allāh ﷻ to let him "share his task" and increase his strength through him.

Stay on the Right Path

"[Allāh] said, "Fear not. Indeed, I am with you both; I hear and I see [everything]."

— *Sūrat Ṭā-Hā (Qur'ān 20:46)*

If you are ever feeling tense or afraid despite being on the right path, remember how Allāh ﷻ comforted his prophets Mūsá (Moses) (PBUH) and Hārūn (Aaron) (PBUH) when they expressed fear that Fir'awn, the powerful and oppressive pharaoh of their time, would punish them if they spoke to him as Allāh commanded.

Do not be afraid; I am with you both, hearing and seeing all that is taking place. That powerful king is only a human being while the almighty and just King of the Universe is by your side.

And so He is with you, O believers...

Allāh, the Most Powerful and the Greatest.

Have trust in Him, and keep your head raised high as you move ahead so long as you are taking the road that pleases Him, the Almighty.

Get a Good Night's Sleep

"[Remember] when He overwhelmed you with drowsiness, as security [descending] from Him..."

— *Sūrat al-Anfāl (Qur'ān 8:11)*

Being able to sleep despite the stress filling your mind is a great blessing from Allāh.

Sleep is very important to maintain good physical and mental health.

It is also what gives you comfort and clarity of thought in order to face whatever difficulties may await you throughout the day.

Allāh ﷻ overwhelmed the believers with drowsiness so they could sleep well right before the big confrontation they were about to have with the disbelievers during the Battle of Badr.

This helped their hearts remain steadfast despite their small numbers in comparison with the large number of the disbelievers.

Whenever you have an important exam, appointment, interview, or whatever...

Remember this verse. Recite it to yourself, and ask Allāh to comfort you with sleep.

And then sleep!

Do not stress yourself with last-minute preparations that your mind has convinced you are necessary. You are most likely already very well prepared, and you should not underestimate the importance of sleep as part of your "preparations" for an important event. As such, do not listen to anyone who tries to make you feel guilty for having a good night's sleep prior to your big day.

Allāh willing, things will go well, and even better than well, with the comfort of Allāh's great blessing that is sleep!

Remind Others of Allāh

"...And he [i.e., Muḥammad ﷺ] said to his companion, 'Do not grieve; indeed Allāh is with us.'"

— Sūrat al-Tawbah (Qur'ān 9:40)

Do not fall into the trap of negativity during difficult times.

Whenever there is fear, sadness, or despair...

Try to always be a source of hope and optimism among others.

Remind your friends and loved ones of Allāh, and say comforting words.

Before you know it, the entire mood will change from one that is sad and gloomy to one that is joyful and positive.

It is a blessing to have righteous friends around you in distressing times. These are the people who will remind you (if you happen to forget) that Allāh is watching over you.

When Prophet Muḥammad ﷺ took shelter in a cave with his closest companion, Abū Bakr al-Ṣiddīq (RA), on their way from Makkah to Madīnah, Abū Bakr (RA) became sad about what might happen to the message of Allāh if the Prophet ﷺ got hurt or captured by the disbelievers.

But the Prophet ﷺ remained calm and comforted his friend, telling him: "Do not grieve; indeed Allāh is with us."

Having trust in Allāh and comforting others with Allāh's words is very important in such situations.

May Allāh ﷻ bless us with kind-hearted companions who offer this type of support and guide us to offer it to others as well.

Do Not Be Distressed by the Arrogant

"No man acts arrogantly or oppressively unless a deficiency is present in his own self."

— Ibn Rushd (d. 1198)

Degrading others and looking down on them has not ever been a strength, nor will it ever be one.

People only do this when they lack self-confidence and faith.

In contrast, a believer is always humble with others—even when he is more knowledgeable or of a higher social status.

Islamic history is rich with authentic stories demonstrating the humbleness of Prophet Muḥammad ﷺ, his esteemed Companions (may Allāh be pleased with them all), and many great Muslim scholars whose knowledge and high status made them even more humble. This is because they recognized that it was only by the will of Allāh ﷻ that they were blessed with such privileges, which they also viewed as responsibilities that should not ever be misused or abused.

If you come across an arrogant man, do not be distressed by him.

He is only revealing his own character flaws and deficiencies, and he will be the only loser if he doesn't take steps to reform himself.

As Allāh ﷻ informs us in a verse from *Sūrat al-Naḥl:*

> "Indeed, He [Allāh] does not like the arrogant."
> *(Qur'ān 16:23)*

Represent Islam as a Faithful Servant

"And the servants of the Most Merciful are those who walk upon the earth easily, and when the ignorant address them [harshly], they say [words of] peace."

— *Sūrat al-Furqān (Qur'ān 25:63)*

My dear believer, if you remain humble and polite despite any arrogance you may encounter in others, you have gained the honor of being a faithful servant of Allāh whom Allāh is pleased with.

Allāh ﷻ has specifically described His servants as those who walk upon the earth "easily," which means that they are gentle, dignified, and do not display arrogance. Even when the ignorant address them harshly, they maintain their calmness, and their words stay "free from fault or evil."[2]

This is because the believers are the humble servants of the Most Merciful.

Imagine if you were the servant of a respected nobleman or king.

Wouldn't you strive to always maintain a high level of professionalism and etiquette regardless of the difficult situations and people you encountered? Even among those who work for (and serve) modern-day government officials and corporate entities, it is well understood that good etiquette helps maintain the good reputation and image of the leader and his or her organization.

But we're not talking about kings, presidents, or CEOs here.

2. https://quranenc.com/ar/browse/english_saheeh/25 (see explanation under Qur'ān 25:63).

We're talking about the Almighty Allāh, Creator of the entire universe!

Is there any honor greater than being a servant of Allāh? And how can we, as Allāh's blessed servants, best represent Islam and show gratitude for all that He has blessed us with in this life?

Bad language and rude or arrogant behavior should never be an option for a faithful servant.

Instead, respond to the ignorant with words of peace so that you may be of those who walk upon the earth easily.

Use Your Body to Perform Good Deeds

"On a Day when their tongues, their hands, and their feet will bear witness against them as to what they used to do."

— Sūrat al-Nūr (Qur'ān 24:24)

It is true that your body is your own body.

But does it really belong to you?

Your organs and other body parts are the creation of Allāh, and any bad deed you engage in while using them is actually at odds with their true purpose, as they were given to you by Allāh to safeguard as you fulfill certain objectives during your short time on Earth.

In addition, any misuse of one's body to commit sins will result in the relevant organ or body part bearing witness against the person who sinned!

So, make a conscious effort to please Allāh through your body's good deeds. Moisten your tongues with the remembrance of Allāh, and use your hands to give charity, help others, and engage in beneficial work. Do not allow your feet to take you anywhere that is not pleasing to Allāh, and protect your eyes and ears from seeing or listening to anything bad.

Never forget that your organs and other body parts are a trust between you and Allāh.

What do you want them to say about you to Allāh ﷻ on the Day of Judgment, when nothing is concealed?

Yet by Allāh's mercy, there are people whose sins will be concealed on the Day of Judgment.

Who are these people? And why? See the next quote.

Conceal the Sins of Others

"A Muslim is the brother of another Muslim; he neither wrongs him, nor does he hand him over to one who does him wrong. If someone fulfills his brother's needs, then Allāh will fulfill his needs; if someone relieves a Muslim of his troubles, then Allāh will relieve his troubles on the Day of Resurrection; and if someone covers up [the sins of] a Muslim, then Allāh will cover up [his sins] on the Day of Resurrection."

— *A saying of Prophet Muḥammad ﷺ (Riyāḍ al-Ṣāliḥīn, No. 244)*

One of Islam's greatest aims is to spread goodness, love, and harmony in society.

If you witness your Muslim brother (or sister) doing something wrong, do not spread rumors or create scandals about this person; instead, advise them privately and conceal their sins and other shortcomings from others.

In other words, "cover him up," as described in the above saying of Prophet Muḥammad ﷺ.

Cover him up, and Allāh will cover your sins! Relieve his troubles, and Allāh will relieve yours!

Of course, we are referring here to people who have sinned privately and not to those who have made proud declarations about their sins in public, encouraging others to commit the same sins. In addition, we are talking about sins that do not affect the rights of others. If someone has committed a crime or caused harm to another person, then it is your duty to speak out or testify so that justice is obtained for the individual who has been wronged or oppressed. This is different than the gossip that many people engage in, which is only for the purpose of "entertainment" and does not actually help anyone.

As Muslims, we should always try to lift each other up and not bring each other down. Remind each other of what is pleasing to Allāh, but in a way that is gentle and appropriate.

Be merciful with others, and Allāh will be merciful with you on the Day of Judgment, *in shā' Allāh.*

Keep Advice Simple and Relatable

"When you speak to people at a level beyond what their minds can grasp, it may become a fitnah [trial] for some."

— *ʾAbd Allāh ibn Masʿūd (RA) (Introduction to Ṣaḥīḥ Muslim)*

Some may feel guilty for not sharing the complex knowledge they have with others who are at a much simpler level.

Ibn Masʿūd (RA) brings attention to a very important matter.

When you preach or give advice to others, you must relate to them, or else it will turn into dispute and dissension among some.

Do not feel guilty for trying to reach out to others with plain, uncomplicated language.

And do not underestimate the efforts of scholars who do the same.

Wisdom, patience, and social intelligence were key traits used by Allāh's prophets (PBUT) to convey the message of Allāh.

Recite the Verses of Tranquility

"Whenever matters became too intense for Shaykh al-Islam Ibn Taymiyyah (may Allāh have mercy on him), he would recite the verses of sakīnah (tranquility)."

— *Ibn al-Qayyim*

The verses of *sakīnah* are six verses from the Qur'ān that mention the concept of tranquility, which is a state of deep contentment that results in inner peace.

A disciple of Ibn Taymiyyah (d. 1328), Ibn al-Qayyim said that he, too, would recite the verses of *sakīnah* (tranquility) when his heart became disturbed over various things. In doing so, he experienced the tremendous effect they had on him, bringing a sense of calm and peace to his heart.

This shows us that the Qur'ān is a remedy for the hearts of the believers.

When your heart is troubled, it is important to isolate yourself a bit from the distractions of this life in order to recite from the Qur'ān and supplicate to Allāh. Do not be like those who seek out the fake pleasures of this world, which damage both the soul and the body, and will thus never provide one's heart with tranquility.

But which verses are the six verses of tranquility?

And what are the components from each verse that have a calming effect on the heart?

Let us take a look at each verse in more detail on the pages that follow. As we will see, the Arabic word *sakīnah* has different shades of meaning depending on the exact context.

Don't Overthink

And their prophet said to them, "Indeed, a sign of his kingship is that the Ark of the Covenant will come to you in which is sakīnah [assurance] from your Lord and a remnant of what the family of Mūsá (Moses) and the family of Hārūn (Aaron) had left, carried by the angels. Indeed in that is a sign for you, if you are believers."

— *Sūrat al-Baqarah (Qur'ān 2:248)*

This verse was revealed in reference to an incident that took place when Banī Isrā'īl (the Israelites) requested from a prophet of theirs to send them a king to help them fight in the cause of Allāh.

But when Allāh sent Ṭālūt (Saul) to be their king, they had doubts and asked:

> "How can he have kingship over us while we are more worthy of kingship than him and he has not been given any measure of wealth?"
> — *Sūrat al-Baqarah (Qur'ān 2:247)*

In response, their prophet reassured them by saying:

> "Indeed, Allāh has chosen him over you and has increased him abundantly in knowledge and stature...."
> — *Sūrat al-Baqarah (Qur'ān 2:247)*

In addition, Allāh ﷻ promised that the Ark of the Covenant, which had been lost to them for many years, would be returned to them as a means of providing them with *sakīnah* (translated to English here as "assurance"), to remove any doubts they may have had from their hearts.

Frequently in our lives, we have doubt about things.

Should I study this major? Is this the right job for me? Is this a good person to marry? What if he or she turns out to be bad? Is this person telling the truth? Am I going to succeed? Does Allāh hear my prayers?

Doubt upon doubt upon doubt...

When this happens to you, try not to overthink. Instead, recite this verse, and ask Allāh ﷻ to reassure you with the blessing of *sakīnah*, and to clear your mind from anything that clouds it.

Pray for Steadfastness

"Then Allāh sent down His sakīnah upon His Messenger and upon the believers and sent down soldiers [i.e., angels] whom you did not see and punished those who disbelieved. And that is the recompense of the disbelievers."

— Sūrat al-Tawbah (Qur'ān 9:26)

Here, *sakīnah* implies the tranquility that comes with being steadfast.

Allāh ﷻ placed steadfastness into the hearts of the believers to remove the fear they experienced after they nearly lost the Battle of Ḥunayn as a test from Allāh, which happened because they were too proud of their great numbers and forgot that victory ultimately comes from Allāh.

It is important to have self-confidence, but never forget that Allāh ﷻ is the one who blessed you with a multitude of factors along the way that resulted in this confidence. The things you achieve in this worldly life are never through your own efforts alone; rather, it is Allāh who makes the road easy for you after you do your best—and if you are ever gripped by fear, it will be difficult to achieve anything.

People are afraid of many different things, and the best remedy for fear is the blessing of *sakīnah*...tranquility from Allāh.

Whenever something is causing your heart to feel unsteady, recite the above verse, and make a sincere supplication to the Almighty Allāh asking Him to send down His tranquility upon you as He did for His Messenger ﷺ and the believers.

Find Comfort in Allāh's Mercy

If you do not aid him [i.e., the Prophet ﷺ] - Allāh has already aided him when those who disbelieved had driven him out [of Makkah] as one of two, when they were in the cave and he [i.e., Muḥammad ﷺ] said to his companion, "Do not grieve; indeed Allāh is with us." And Allāh sent down His sakīnah upon him and supported him with soldiers [i.e., angels] you did not see and made the word of those who disbelieved the lowest, while the word of Allāh - that is the highest. And Allāh is Exalted in Might and Wise."

— Sūrat al-Tawbah (Qur'ān 9:40)

This verse of the Qur'ān illustrates the beautiful way in which Allāh ﷻ sends down His *sakīnah* upon us in times of hardship and distress. The calming effect this tranquility has upon the heart is a form of mercy that allows us to sense the presence and support of Allāh during our most difficult moments.

Whenever you feel emotions like loneliness, fear, or hopelessness, remember that Allāh is always with you no matter where you are.

Allāh cares about you—and He will send down His tranquility upon you.

Hold on to your faith, and remember to ask the Generous Allāh whose mercy encompasses all things for the mercy of His *sakīnah* whenever you recite the above verse.

Draw Closer to Allāh

"It is He who sent down sakīnah into the hearts of the believers that they would increase in faith along with their [present] faith. And to Allāh belong the soldiers of the heavens and the earth, and ever is Allāh Knowing and Wise."

— Sūrat al-Fatḥ (Qur'ān 48:4)

Did you know?

Having faith results in the blessing of *sakīnah* (tranquility) from Allāh that increases your faith even more!

This reminds me of a powerful ḥadīth narrated by Prophet Muḥammad ﷺ, who said the following words:

> "Allāh says: 'When a servant of Mine draws near to Me the span of a palm, I draw near to him a cubit; and if he draws near to Me a cubit, I draw near to him the span of two outstretched arms. And if he comes to Me walking, I go to him running.'"
> *(Riyāḍ al-Ṣāliḥīn, No. 96)*

So, have faith in Allāh. The closer you draw to Him, the closer He draws to you. The more tranquility you receive from Him, the more faith you will have as well.

Gain Tranquility Through Your Good Deeds

"Certainly was Allāh pleased with the believers when they pledged allegiance to you, [O Muḥammad], under the tree, and He knew what was in their hearts, so He sent down sakīnah upon them and rewarded them with an imminent conquest."

— Sūrat al-Fatḥ (Qur'ān 48:18)

Having good, pure intentions that are reflected in your actions means that you will definitely be rewarded by Allāh. Among the many blessings you may gain is the *sakīnah* (tranquility) He sends down upon the believers to show He is pleased with them.

Do not underestimate the value of your good deeds.

Whenever you recite the above verse, remember all of the good things you have done purely for Allāh's sake. Then ask Allāh to accept your good intentions and bless you with the mercy of His tranquility.

Find Guidance Through Tranquility

"[Remember] when those who disbelieved had filled their hearts with pride - the pride of [pre-Islamic] ignorance. But Allāh sent down His sakīnah upon His Messenger and upon the believers and imposed upon them the word of righteousness, and they were more deserving of it and worthy of it. And ever is Allāh, of all things, Knowing."

— *Sūrat al-Fatḥ (Qur'ān 48:26)*

Earlier in this book, we saw how the faithful servants of Allāh remain gentle and dignified in the face of adversity, using wisdom and diplomacy to solve problems.

In the above verse, Allāh ﷻ informs us that it is because He sent down His *sakīnah* (tranquility) upon His Messenger ﷺ and the believers that they knew exactly how to handle a difficult situation, staying strong so that they could continue to deliver the message of Islam.

Tranquility from Allāh gives one the wisdom and calmness needed to deal with difficulties. It is this tranquility that helps guide us to the right path that pleases Allāh.

Whenever you are overwhelmed, stop for a moment to recite this verse. Then ask Allāh ﷻ to send His tranquility upon you so that you can take the road that pleases Him.

My dear reader, calmness of the heart is a very important blessing from Allāh that helps one attain good mental, physical, and spiritual health. Now that you know about the six verses of tranquility, ponder upon the meaning of each one, and hold fast to what you have learned.

Respond to Allāh

"And when My servants ask you, [O Muḥammad], concerning Me - indeed I am near. I respond to the invocation of the supplicant when he calls upon Me. So let them respond to Me [by obedience] and believe in Me that they may be [rightly] guided."

— *Sūrat al-Baqarah (Qur'ān 2:186)*

Allāh ﷻ tells us in the above verse of the Qur'ān that He is near, something which we find mentioned in *Sūrat Qāf* as well:

> "And We have already created man and know what his soul whispers to him, and We are closer to him than [his] jugular vein."
> *(Qur'ān 50:16)*

The wording here indicates that Allāh ﷻ has absolute knowledge about you that no one else possesses; He is closer to you than your own jugular vein!

As such, we don't need a mediator to speak to Allāh, nor do we need to raise our voices when seeking a favor from Allāh, The Most Generous. He is near—much nearer than we can imagine.

He hears and knows everything we are asking for, and He will respond when called upon.

In turn, we too must respond to Allāh, and this is done by believing in Him and showing obedience to His commands. This is so that we may be rightly guided, as the verse indicates.

Have Taqwá

"O you who have believed, if you fear Allāh, He will grant you a criterion and will remove from you your misdeeds and forgive you. And Allāh is the possessor of great bounty."

— *Sūrat al-Anfāl (Qur'ān 8:29)*

Dear believer, if you wish to be guided (which includes having the ability to distinguish between truth and falsehood), you first have to fear Allāh.

Not only will you be guided, but you will also be forgiven for your sins and shortcomings.

A heart that fears Allāh shall never be let down.

Fear of Allāh is known in Arabic as *taqwá*, which ʿAlī ibn Abī Ṭālib (RA) described as "fear of *al-Jalīl* [Allāh], acting upon *al-tanzīl* [the Qurʾān], being content with *qalīl* [little], and being prepared for the Day of *Raḥīl* [departure from this life]."

But how is being content with little considered a form of *taqwá*?

Read on to find out.

Be Content with Little

"And [remember] when your Lord proclaimed, 'If you are grateful, I will surely increase you [in favor]; but if you deny, indeed, My punishment is severe.'"

— *Sūrat Ibrāhīm (Qur'ān 14:7)*

Being content with little is part of being grateful to Allāh, and being grateful to Allāh is part of believing in Allāh, as the opposite of gratitude is associated with *kufr* in the original Arabic verse, which is disbelief in (and denial of) Allāh.

Of course, being content with the simpler things in life does not necessarily mean one should not strive for more; it just means that we should not underestimate what we already have (no matter how little), as the seemingly "small" things in life are all blessings provided to us by the Creator.

When we recognize this and show gratitude to Allāh for all of His blessings, big and small alike, He will surely increase us in favor and bless us even more.

So, always make the best out of what you have and remember to thank Allāh. He will bless you in return!

Show Kindness to Parents

"...Be grateful to Me [Allāh] and to your parents; to Me is the [final] destination."

— Sūrat Luqmān (Qur'ān 31:14)

Allāh ﷻ associates gratitude to Him with gratitude to one's parents.

As we have seen, thanking Allāh shows faith in Allāh—and one way to thank Allāh is by thanking our parents...for raising us, for taking care of us, and for all of the sacrifices they have made on our behalf.

Allāh ﷻ gives huge importance to parents in several verses in the Qur'ān. We must honor them and show kindness to them even if they do not share the same beliefs.

> "But if they [your parents] endeavor to make you associate with Me [Allāh] that of which you have no knowledge, do not obey them but accompany them in [this] world with appropriate kindness..."
> *— Sūrat Luqmān (Qur'ān 31:15)*

No matter the situation, we must always strive to be kind and respectful to our parents.

As Allāh ﷻ tells us in a verse from *Sūrat al-Isrā':*

> "...Say not to them [so much as], 'uff,' and do not repel them but speak to them a noble word."
> *(Qur'ān 17:23)*

"Uff" is an expression of irritation that one may sometimes feel toward another person, but we must avoid expressing ourselves this way with our parents.

Pleasing our parents means pleasing Allāh—and it is crucial for our success in both this life and the Hereafter.

Pray for a Righteous Family

"And those who say, 'Our Lord! Grant us [pious] spouses and offspring who will be a comfort to our eyes, and make us models for the righteous.' Those will be awarded the Chamber for what they patiently endured, and they will be received therein with greetings and [words of] peace."

— Sūrat al-Furqān (Qur'ān 25:74–75)

This passage from the Qur'ān contains a great *du'ā'* (supplication) one should make for the blessing of righteous spouses and children. The very act of making this supplication is a good deed that appears among a list of other good deeds in the verses prior to it that will result in a great reward called the "Chamber," which is the most elevated portion of Paradise and a very beautiful place beyond what anyone can imagine.

In this *du'ā'*, you should also ask Allāh ﷻ to make you yourself among the righteous so that you may be a good example for others.

These are blessings that Allāh grants to His favored servants—so always make *du'ā'* to be among them.

This can be achieved by staying on the right path and always striving to implant the seeds of faith into the hearts of your children. Likewise, make sure to choose a good spouse who will support you as you raise your children in a way that is pleasing to Allāh.

Understand Your Limitations

"He said, 'O Nūḥ, indeed he is not of your family; indeed, he is [one whose] work was other than righteous, so ask Me not for that about which you have no knowledge. Indeed, I advise you, lest you be among the ignorant.'"

— *Sūrat Hūd (Qur'ān 11:46)*

Despite our desire for righteous spouses and children, Allāh ﷻ informs us that sometimes things don't work out the way we hoped.

It may be that you are a righteous servant of Allāh who does everything possible to be a positive influence on your family—but in the end someone in your household chooses a different path.

This could be for many reasons, including outside influences such as friends or online temptations. Some may sadly even become arrogant and refuse any advice or good words that remind them of Allāh ﷻ, coming to regard their own parents, siblings, and spouses as enemies.

Prophet Nūḥ (Noah) (PBUH) was saddened by the fact that his son chose to be among the wrongdoers despite all of his father's attempts to remind him of Allāh—and remember! Nūḥ (PBUH) wasn't just a righteous father; he was a prophet as well.

Nūḥ (PBUH) called upon Allāh ﷻ, saying:

> "My Lord, indeed my son is of my family."
> — *Sūrat Hūd (Qur'ān 11:45)*

But Allāh ﷻ informed him that this was not the case.

"Indeed he is not of your family; indeed, he is [one whose] work was other than righteous..."

As painful as these situations are, this verse serves to comfort the believers about an all-too-common reality.

Yes, you should continue to offer your loved ones advice and do everything you can to help them remain on a path that is pleasing to Allāh ﷻ, but what others choose is ultimately not in your hands.

It is between them and Allāh.

As Allāh ﷻ informed Prophet Muḥammad ﷺ (and us) in a verse from *Sūrat al-Qaṣaṣ:*

> "Indeed, [O Muḥammad], you do not guide whom you like, but Allāh guides whom He wills. And He is most knowing of the [rightly] guided."
> *(Qur'ān 28:56)*

O Allāh! Guide us, and guide our loved ones, too.

Strive to Be of the Righteous

"Gardens of perpetual residence; they will enter them with whoever were righteous among their forefathers, their spouses and their descendants. And the angels will enter upon them from every gate."

— *Sūrat al-Raʿd (Qurʾān 13:23)*

Here, Allāh ﷻ is basically telling us that it is only the righteous who will attain Paradise.

If the members of your family were righteous as well, then they will accompany you, *in shāʾ Allāh.*

Otherwise, the type of family one comes from makes no difference. A nobleman is no better than a person of a more humble background; what matters to Allāh ﷻ is our individual deeds.

We see this clearly in a verse from *Sūrat al-Taḥrīm:*

> "Allāh presents an example of those who disbelieved: the wife of Nūḥ (Noah) and the wife of Lūṭ (Lot). They were under two of Our righteous servants but betrayed them, so they [i.e., those prophets] did not avail them from Allāh at all, and it was said, 'Enter the Fire with those who enter.'" *(Qurʾān 66:10)*

Despite their status as the wives of prophets, the wives of Nūḥ and Lūṭ (PBUT) chose the wrong path and did not repent to Allāh; as such, their destiny was to enter Hellfire. As the verse indicates, it didn't matter how righteous their husbands were.

A person can only be admitted to Paradise on the basis of his or her own merits.

If, on the other hand, someone was the only righteous member of his or her household, then this will not prevent the person from entering Paradise, as was the case with the believing wife of Firʿawn, the oppressive pharaoh who lived at the time of Prophet Mūsá (Moses) (PBUH).

> "And Allāh presents an example of those who believed: the wife of Pharaoh, when she said, 'My Lord, build for me near You a house in Paradise and save me from Firʿawn and his deeds and save me from the wrongdoing people.'"
> — *Sūrat al-Taḥrīm (Qur'ān 66:11)*

Remember, it doesn't matter who you are related to in this worldly life.

As Allāh ﷻ tells us in a verse from *Sūrat al-Ḥujurāt:*

> "Indeed, the most noble of you in the sight of Allāh is the most righteous of you."
> *(Qur'ān 49:13)*

And this is what will be of most importance on the Day of Judgment.

Turn to Allāh

"So he invoked his Lord, 'Indeed, I am overpowered, so help.'"

— *Sūrat al-Qamar (Qur'ān 54:10)*

This heartfelt quote from the Qur'ān appears in the story of Prophet Nūḥ (Noah) (PBUH).

Prophet Nūḥ (PBUH) preached the message of *tawḥīd* (belief in One God) to his people for many long years, yet they kept calling him a "madman," while only a few who were among the righteous chose to follow the right path.

Life can get very hard, and you may undergo tough situations in which you literally lose everything, including your own spirit.

This is when you have to turn to Allāh and make *du'ā'*.

In a passage from *Sūrat al-Shu'arā' (Qur'ān 26:77–82)*, we find Prophet Ibrāhīm (Abraham) (PBUH) describing Allāh ﷻ, the Lord of the Worlds, as He who created him, guided him, fed him, provided him with drink, and cured him whenever he was ill. He further says that it is Allāh who will cause him to die and then bring him back to life, and that it is Allāh whom he hopes will forgive him for his sins on the Day of Recompense.

Such is Allāh ﷻ to every single soul in this universe.

In other words, He is the One in whose hands is everything. He is there for you in all situations you may face, and He will help you get through the difficulties of this life. Just turn to Him with all of your heart and soul.

For another example regarding this issue from the Qur'ān, let's take a look at the story of Prophet Ayūb (Job) (PBUH).

Remain Steadfast in Times of Adversity

"And [mention] Ayūb, when he called to his Lord, 'Indeed, adversity has touched me, and You are the most merciful of the merciful.' So We responded to him and removed what afflicted him of adversity. And We gave him [back] his family and the like thereof with them as mercy from Us and a reminder for the worshipers [of Allāh]."

— Sūrat al-Anbiyā' (Qur'ān 21:83–84)

Prophet Ayūb (Job) (PBUH) was not only tested with a severe illness, but he also had to be away from his family.

One can imagine how difficult this was, yet Prophet Ayūb (PBUH) remained patient for a long time—and when he asked Allāh ﷻ to help him, he asked him respectfully and humbly.

He didn't get mad at his Lord or express frustration or resentment as people sometimes do in such situations, forgetting that part of life's many tests is the ability to maintain faith in the face of adversity.

He did not go seeking help from others, and he did not despair. He called Allāh "the most merciful of the merciful."

And Allāh ﷻ answered Ayūb's *du'ā'*, making mention of his good qualities:

> "Indeed, We found him patient, an excellent servant. Indeed, he was one repeatedly turning back [to Allāh]."
> *— Sūrat Ṣād (Qur'ān 38:44)*

Allāh ﷻ preserved this story as a reminder to us, the worshipers of Allāh, that tough situations do happen in this life, but Allāh is merciful and will remove the affliction, comfort us, heal us, and compensate us.

So, make *duʿā*ʾ, and do not despair. Trust in Allāh.

But should we only make *duʿā*ʾ when times are difficult?

Read on to find out what Prophet Muḥammad ﷺ said about this matter.

Supplicate During Times of Ease

"Whoever wishes that Allāh would respond to him during hardship and grief, then let him supplicate plentifully when at ease."

— A saying of Prophet Muḥammad ﷺ (Jāmiʿ al-Tirmidhī, No. 3382)

As Muslims, we should always make *duʿā'*, no matter the situation. This includes during times of happiness, sadness, ease, and hardship.

In addition, our supplications can be made almost anywhere, whether we are taking a walk, riding on the bus, washing the dishes, or drifting off to sleep.

Duʿā' is not just for the purpose of asking for a favor or removing an affliction. *Duʿā'* is how we talk to Allāh, which makes it a means of connecting to Allāh and getting close to Him in every circumstance.

Among other things, *duʿā'* includes thanking Allāh for His many blessings. When we make *duʿā'*, we show love for the Creator by asking Him to guide us to the path that is most pleasing to Him. The very act of making *duʿā'* means we have trust in Allāh and recognize His Authority. In return, Allāh ﷻ loves His faithful servants who make *duʿā'*—and He also loves to answer their supplications and prayers.

Prophet Muḥammad ﷺ said:

> "Your Lord is Modest and Generous, and He loathes to turn away a servant of His emptyhanded when he raises his hands up to Him [in supplication]."
> *(Recorded in Bulūgh al-Marām)*

In many verses of the Qur'ān, Allāh ﷻ tells us that He will respond to our *du'ā'*. He also tells us the stories of the prophets and shows us how they used to make *du'ā'* in different circumstances, including during times of ease. One example of this is found when Prophet Sulaymān (Solomon) (PBUH) heard an ant saying:

> "O ants, enter your dwellings that you not be crushed by Sulaymān and his soldiers while they perceive not."
> — *Sūrat al-Naml (Qur'ān 27:18)*

Prophet Sulaymān (PBUH) then "...smiled, amused at her speech, and said:

> 'My Lord, enable me to be grateful for Your favor which You have bestowed upon me and upon my parents and to do righteousness of which You approve. And admit me by Your mercy into [the ranks of] Your righteous servants.'"
> — *Sūrat al-Naml (Qur'ān 27:19)*

Recognize Allāh's Plan for You

"And know that if the people were to gather together to benefit you with anything, they would not benefit you except with what Allāh has already prescribed for you. And if they were to gather together to harm you with anything, they would not harm you except with what Allāh has already prescribed against you."

— A saying of Prophet Muḥammad ﷺ (Al-Nawawī's Forty Ḥadīth, No. 19)

This is a reminder that everything that happens in this life happens by the will of Allāh alone, whether it is a blessing, a lesson, or a test.

That's why we shouldn't worry too much about what the people around us do or don't do.

If Allāh has decreed for you to have something, then you will have it no matter what, regardless of any envy or bad intentions concealed in people's hearts.

No one can ever harm you when the Almighty Allāh is protecting you.

This reminder from the Prophet ﷺ is a part of a longer narration that teaches us exactly how to cultivate this level of trust and belief. Among other things, Prophet Muḥammad ﷺ advised us to always be mindful of Allāh ﷻ, and to seek help from Him alone. In a similar narration, we are advised to recognize and acknowledge Allāh in times of ease and prosperity so that He may remember us in times of adversity. The Prophet ﷺ also said:

> "And know that with patience comes victory, with affliction comes relief, and with hardship comes ease."
> *(Recorded in Al-Nawawī's Forty Ḥadīth, No. 19)*

Be Mindful of the Present

"Man's feet will not move on the Day of Resurrection before he is asked about his life [and how he consumed it]."

— *A saying of Prophet Muḥammad ﷺ (Riyāḍ al-Ṣāliḥīn, No. 407)*

Every new day we are alive is a new beginning and a blessing from Allāh that gives us the opportunity to change our lives for the better.

So many people spend countless hours grieving over the past to the extent that they forget to live the present, not realizing that it, too, will soon turn into the past, and that Allāh ﷻ will ask us about all of the time we "consumed" during our short time on Earth.

It is true one can't return to the past, but today and tomorrow are always filled with new possibilities. There is always something new and positive we can do, such as helping more people with their needs or starting a beneficial project. Even just bringing a smile to someone's face for a brief moment is a praiseworthy deed that can make a real difference in that person's day.

The secret to having a positive outlook toward the present is to maintain our faith and find contentment in what Allāh has prescribed for us. In addition, acting upon the blessing of time will elevate our status with Allāh, making us among the people whom Allāh is pleased with on the Day of Judgment.

Don't Expect Perfection from Others

"And live with them in kindness. For if you dislike them - perhaps you dislike a thing and Allāh makes therein much good."

— Sūrat al-Nisā' (Qur'ān 4:19)

This verse of the Qur'ān talks about trying to overlook the flaws you dislike in your spouse, as you may find a lot of other things that you do like.

Trying to stay on the right path by choosing good friends and a pious spouse does not mean that you should expect others to be perfect, as you yourself are not perfect, nor will you ever be.

As Muslims, we try our best to be good and to have a positive impact on others.

But a big part of faith is learning to accept people's flaws—overlooking their shortcomings and not being overly judgmental.

Every human being on Earth has positive qualities, so why disregard this and focus on the negatives?

If we focus solely on other people's imperfections, we will definitely spend our lives in perpetual loneliness—and Islam was never meant to encourage a solitary existence.

It is completely the opposite, as Islam teaches us how to live with people and have successful relationships despite our differences and imperfections.

It is completely normal to have differences and occasional disagreements, but the most important thing is that we work things out in a way that is pleasing to Allāh ﷻ.

Dealing nicely with others and showing mercy toward them within the boundaries of Islam will result in Allāh having mercy with us as well.

Prophet Muḥammad ﷺ said:

> "The merciful are shown mercy by al-Raḥmān [The Most Merciful]. Be merciful on the earth, and you will be shown mercy from He Who is above the heavens...."
> *(Jāmiʿ al-Tirmidhī, No. 1924)*

Set Realistic Goals

"The acts most pleasing to Allāh are those which are done continuously, even if they are small."

— A saying of Prophet Muḥammad ﷺ (Ṣaḥīḥ Muslim)

It is a great thing when someone wishes to change his or her life for the better.

Yet many people start off with feelings of motivation and excitement only to become deflated within a short period of time. This often happens when a person has not set realistic goals that can be comfortably achieved in a gradual manner. Pretty soon, they give up.

If you wish to achieve a goal, first break it down into smaller steps that are easier to manage.

Aim to make changes you can do continuously even if they seem relatively minor or insignificant.

Be realistic, and have patience.

With time, you will be able to achieve more, *in shā' Allāh.*

Make Your Days Count

"If the Final Hour comes while you have the sapling of a plant in your hands and it is possible to plant it before the Hour comes, you should plant it."

— A saying of Prophet Muḥammad ﷺ (Al-Adab al-Mufrad)

The urgent message conveyed to us here is that every single minute in our lives counts! So, make your days count by filling them with good deeds.

It's not enough to be believers in our hearts.

One should strive to make the world a better place using the capacities and special traits given to him by Allāh.

Always ask yourself: What is something I can do to make people's lives a little easier? What type of things might help generate positive energy that inspires others?

It doesn't necessarily have to be something big; it could be as simple as planting trees in your neighborhood, providing seats in a public place where people stand for a long time, writing a book that you always wished to read, or saying a good word to whomever you meet.

In addition, make time to share ideas and have meaningful conversations with the people around you. It is also important to laugh and have fun with your friends and loved ones! This alone is a means of worshiping Allāh and showing gratitude for the time He has given you surrounded by the people you love.

There is always something positive you can do, within your own capacity.

This is how you give back to this world and make your days count, adding to your record of good deeds on the Day of Judgment, *in shā' Allāh.*

Plan for Everlasting Rewards

"When a man dies, his deeds come to an end except for three: ṣadaqah jāriyah (ongoing charity); knowledge which is beneficial; or a virtuous descendant who prays for him."

— A saying of Prophet Muḥammad ﷺ (Riyāḍ al-Ṣāliḥīn, No. 1383)

The Prophet ﷺ is telling us here that a person can still be rewarded for his good deeds even after death. It all depends on what we left behind in this world.

These everlasting rewards are found in three key things: charity that people continue to benefit from (such as the establishment of a well or school); beneficial knowledge that you pass on to others; and a righteous descendant who prays for you after you are gone.

One should keep this in mind and aim to have at least one deed that continues to please Allāh after his or her death.

In addition, if someone dear to you has died, don't ever stop praying for him.

You may be the remaining deed that continues to reward this person after he is gone from this world.

Have Faith in Allāh's Love for You

"And spend in the way of Allāh and do not throw [yourselves] with your [own] hands into destruction [by refraining]. And do good; indeed, Allāh loves the doers of good."

— *Sūrat al-Baqarah (Qur'ān 2:195)*

Do not throw yourself into a state of destruction, for Allāh ﷻ loves you and wants the best for you and all of humanity.

A popular story regarding this topic states that a righteous woman once served as a family maid in a home, and she had the good fortune of being among those who prayed late at night (when everyone else was asleep). One night, it happened that the man of the house heard the woman speaking to Allāh as she prostrated during her prayers. "O Allāh!" she called out. "I beseech of You with Your love for me to honor me with more *taqwá* [piety]!"

So, when she was finished praying, the man asked her, "How can you be so sure that Allāh loves you? Shouldn't you have said 'O Allāh, I beseech of You with my love for You' instead?"

To this, the woman replied, "If Allāh hadn't loved me, He would not have woken me up this hour, and if He hadn't loved me, He wouldn't have let me stand before Him, and if He hadn't loved me, He wouldn't have allowed me to relay this private conversation to you now."

My dear reader, you may have experienced incidents in your life when you felt compelled to go out of your way to do a good deed without really understanding what inspired you to do it.

It is actually Allāh who guided you, because He loves you and desires for you to be rewarded.

The righteous woman in this story understood this secret and had enough confidence to express what she believed in her heart to be true during the supplications of her night prayers.

Some may feel that it is inappropriate to express this level of confidence in Allāh's love. After all, how can we be sure that Allāh ﷻ really loves us?

We know because of His blessed guidance!

The Creator loves every single one of us and wants us to choose the right path so that we may gain the rewards of both this life and the Hereafter. Without Allāh's guidance, we would undoubtedly be lost—so have faith in Allāh's love for you, and always strive to take the path that is most pleasing to Him.

CHERISH YOUR FATHER

"One's father is the middle door of Paradise [i.e., the best path to Paradise], so it is up to you whether you take advantage of it or not."

— A saying of Prophet Muḥammad ﷺ (Sunan Ibn Mājah, No. 3663)

Having a father is a great blessing from Allāh. This is a person who loves you more than he loves his own self—even if he never utters these words aloud.

Your good relationship with your father will grant you the best path to Paradise, so be humble with the man who raised you. Respect him, cherish him, and help him in any way you can.

Even if you disagree with your father on occasion, avoid harsh words and pointless arguments, as such conflicts can only lead to feelings of hurt and resentment on both sides. Learn to have patience by taking Prophet Ibrāhīm (Abraham) (PBUH) as your example.

When the father of Prophet Ibrāhīm (PBUH) refused to worship Allāh ﷻ and let go of his false gods, Ibrāhīm (PBUH) was still kind and respectful to him despite the fact that his father had threatened to stone him if he didn't stop preaching to him.

In response, Prophet Ibrāhīm (PBUH) only said the following:

> "Peace [i.e., safety] will be upon you. I will ask forgiveness for you of my Lord. Indeed, He is ever gracious to me."
> *— Sūrat Maryam (Qur'ān 19:47)*

Fathers are special; that's why Allāh ﷻ made it incumbent upon us to give them good treatment. By acknowledging their special status and recognizing their hard work along with the many good things they have done for us throughout our lives, we will have a special reward from Allāh ﷻ.

In the end, remember the words of ʿAbd Allāh ibn ʿUmar (RA), the famous son of ʿUmar ibn al-Khaṭṭāb (RA) who was also a beloved Companion of Prophet Muḥammad ﷺ:

> "The pleasure of the Lord lies in the pleasure of the father, and the displeasure of the Lord lies in the displeasure of the father."
> *(Al-Adab al-Mufrad, No. 2)*

Cherish Your Mother

"And [Allāh made me] dutiful to my mother, and He has not made me a wretched tyrant."

— *Sūrat Maryam (Qur'ān 19:32)*

By Allāh's miracle, these were among the first words Prophet ʿĪsá (Jesus) (PBUH) spoke as a newborn baby while still in the cradle.

Note that he linked being kind to his mother with being humble to Allāh.

The fact that this was among his first statements highlights how important it is.

If you are a good person, then you must be dutiful to your mother.

Being dutiful to your mother distinguishes you as a good person.

Respect her, help her, and do not be grouchy with her.

Remember that she carried you with hardship and gave birth to you with hardship—yet she was fully devoted to taking care of you throughout all stages of your life.

She is the one who will always love you and support you.

Mothers are a great blessing from Allāh that has no equal, so do not ever abuse this blessing.

Instead, show appreciation for all of the good things your mother has taught you.

Doing so will help make your journey in life more meaningful and add to your register of good deeds in the Hereafter, *in shāʾ Allāh.*

Repel Evil with Goodness

"And not equal are the good deed and the bad. Repel [evil] by that [deed] which is better; and thereupon, the one whom between you and him is enmity [will become] as though he was a devoted friend."

— *Sūrat Fuṣṣilat (Qur'ān 41:34)*

Some people can't wait to get revenge from those who have treated them badly.

But it is almost always better to treat such people better than they have treated you.

If we do this for the sake of Allāh ﷻ, we cut off the path to evil and create a new dynamic.

In many cases, your good treatment of the people who have hurt you will help them rethink what they have done, and this may be the thing that actually helps them stop their hurtful behaviors. When this is achieved, goodness and harmony flourish in society.

Yet, in order to obtain this result, one must be patient and devout to Allāh, as indicated in the next verse:

> "But none is granted it except those who are patient, and none is granted it except one having a great portion [of good]."
> — *Sūrat Fuṣṣilat (Qur'ān 41:35)*

Make Others Happy

"Allāh helps His servant as long as His servant helps his brother."

— A saying of Prophet Muḥammad ﷺ (Ṣaḥīḥ Muslim)

You only stand to gain when you are busy performing good deeds and doing what you can to help others and make them happy.

Allāh's guardianship will surround you from every side.

Allāh ﷻ always sends good people to help those who are kind to others, relieving their hardships with His infinite mercy as a sign that He is pleased with them.

So, always be kind, smile to others, and bring ease to people's affairs as much as you can. You will undoubtedly receive the same (and much more!) in return—in both this life and in the Hereafter.

Restrain Anger

"[The righteous] ... who restrain anger and who pardon the people—and Allāh loves al-muḥsinīn [the doers of good]."

— *Sūrat Āli 'Imrān (Qur'ān 3:134)*

In this verse of the Qur'ān, we learn about *al-muḥsinīn* (the doers of good), which is a description of the righteous derived from the Arabic word *al-iḥsān.*

Al-iḥsān is the highest rank of faith. When asked to define it, Prophet Muḥammad ﷺ said it means:

> "To worship Allāh as if you see Him, for even if you cannot see Him, He sees you."
> *(Ṣaḥīḥ al-Bukhārī, No. 50)*

To restrain anger when things are tense requires one to have a high level of patience, discipline, and self-control—but if one always worships Allāh while striving for *iḥsān*, things become much easier.

Prophet Muḥammad ﷺ taught his Companions (may Allāh be pleased with them all) different ways of restraining anger, including the following:

> "If one of you is angry while he is standing, let him sit down so his anger will leave him; otherwise, let him lie down."
> *(Sunan Abī Dā'ūd, No. 4782)*

He also said, "When you are angry, be silent." He repeated this twice. *(Al-Adab al-Mufrad, No. 1320)*

Another reminder from the Prophet ﷺ states that:

> "A strong man is not one who physically overpowers others. A strong man is one who controls himself when he is angry."
> *(Al-Adab al-Mufrad, No. 1317)*

People who follow this advice are among the *muḥsinīn*—the doers of good whom Allāh loves.

Seek Relief in Prayer

Ḥudhayfah*[3] *said: "When anything distressed the Prophet ﷺ, he prayed."

— *Sunan Abī Dā'ūd, No. 1319*

Prayer is the best remedy for distress.

It brings clarity to the mind and comforts your heart and soul, reminding you that everything in this world is small compared to the greatness of Allāh.

Other than the five obligatory prayers in Islam, there are other (supererogatory) prayers one can pray when times are difficult or stressful.

First there is *Ṣalāt al-Ḥājah* (The Prayer of Need), which includes a special supplication to remove distress. Another important prayer is *Ṣalāt al-Istikhārah* (The Prayer of Seeking Counsel), which one prays to ask Allāh for guidance and certainty when making big decisions in life.

Never abandon your prayers, for they are a lifeline between you and Allāh ﷻ—a special connection you have with the Creator that can help resolve all of your pain, worries, and distress.

3. Ḥudhayfah ibn al-Yamān (RA), a Companion of Prophet Muḥammad ﷺ.

Love for the Sake of Allāh

"By Allāh, their faces will glow, and they will be (sitting) in (pulpits of) light. They will have no fear (on the Day) when the people will have fear, and they will not grieve when the people will grieve."

— *A saying of Prophet Muḥammad ﷺ (Sunan Abī Dā'ūd, No. 3527)*

This is a description of the "allies" of Allāh, who will have a magnificent reward in the Hereafter. But let us take a look at the full ḥadīth to understand who these allies of Allāh actually are.

> "There are people among the servants of Allāh who are neither prophets nor martyrs; the prophets and martyrs will admire them on the Day of Resurrection due to their position before the Almighty Allāh."
>
> They (the people) asked: "O Messenger of Allāh, tell us who are they are."
>
> He replied: "They are people who love one another with the spirit of Allāh, despite having no shared family relations or (monetary interests) together. By Allāh, their faces will glow, and they will be (sitting) in (pulpits of) light. They will have no fear (on the Day) when the people will have fear, and they will not grieve when the people will grieve."
>
> He (the Prophet ﷺ) then recited the following Qur'ānic verse: "Unquestionably, [for] the allies of Allāh there will be no fear concerning them, nor will they grieve."[4]

4. *Sūrat Yūnus (Qur'ān 10:62)*

As we can see, these blessed people are those who love one another for the sake of Allāh!

But what does it mean to love one another for the sake of Allāh?

First, it is recognizing that the person you love is a servant of Allāh, just like you are. No matter how unique or special this person is, remember that it is Allāh ﷻ Who blessed this person with his or her special traits.

Second, your relationship should not be one that is based on worldly interests. It should instead be based on wanting what is good for each other according to what is pleasing to Allāh.

Third, you always make *du'ā'* for each other. You remind each other to stay on the right path, and you never take part in *ḥarām* (prohibited) activities when you are together.

Fourth, if the other person goes astray, you help him or her return to the right path that is pleasing to Allāh.

Fifth, if the person decides to continue on the wrong path despite the good advice he or she has been given, it is often better to part ways until the matter is rectified, because the ties between you are for Allāh's sake alone, and these ties cease to exist once a servant insists on straying from the path of righteousness. Yet you should always make *du'ā'* for the one who is astray, as this person may someday come back to the right path.

Rely on Allāh

"A strong believer is better and dearer to Allāh than a weak one, and both are good. Adhere to that which is beneficial for you. Keep asking Allāh for help and do not refrain from it. If you are afflicted in any way, do not say: 'If I had taken this or that step, it would have resulted into such and such,' but say only: 'Allāh so determined and did as He willed.' The word 'if' opens the gates of satanic thoughts."

— *A saying of Prophet Muḥammad ﷺ (Riyāḍ al-Ṣāliḥīn, No. 100)*

Islam gives us the keys to achieving self-confidence, certainty, and a positive attitude.

It is by having faith in Allāh.

Unlike the popular trends of our time, you don't need to take courses on how to believe in the power of your subconscious mind, nor do you need to start meditating or continuously trying to convince yourself that you have unlimited power that allows you to control every single situation you are in.

You just need to do your best and then rely on Allāh ﷻ to make everything easy and give you confidence, strength, and certainty.

In other words, you just need to trust in Allāh!

Think about it for a moment. Why would you go seek out the powers of others to improve yourself when you are already connected to the main source of power on this earth (and in this universe)?

Understanding and following the advice of the Prophet ﷺ helps free one from the shackles of weakness, laziness, negativity, and fear. You cannot be plagued by feelings of inferiority or doubt when you know that Allāh ﷻ is by your side, and that He is helping you to be firm, strong, and confident.

Do Not Grieve Over Hurtful Words

"And let not their speech grieve you. Indeed, honor [due to power] belongs to Allāh entirely. He is the Hearing, the Knowing."

— Sūrat Yūnus (Qur'ān 10:65)

If you are like most people, there will be times in life when people say hurtful things, even when all you say on your part are good words and positive things that are pleasing to Allāh.

They may insult you, tell lies about you, or even blackmail you. Let not their speech grieve you.

This is what Allāh ﷻ told Prophet Muḥammad ﷺ fourteen centuries ago.

This verse now serves as a reminder for the believers.

No matter how mean, hurtful, or false another person's words are, they can never be strong.

All the power is with Allāh—and He hears and knows everything. Do not grieve.

Turn Away from the Ignorant

"Take what is given freely, enjoin what is good, and turn away from the ignorant."

— Sūrat al-Aʿrāf (Qur'ān 7:199)

This verse from the Qurʾān provides simple guidance from Allāh ﷻ on how to treat people.

Take whatever good they offer you, accept their apologies, and do not delve too deeply into their true intentions. Assume the best whenever possible.

Be easygoing, and give good advice.

But if you encounter someone who causes harm and can't be reasoned with, then simply turn away from him.

Do not go down to the same level.

Help the Oppressed

"A Muslim is the brother of a Muslim; he does not oppress him, nor does he fail him, nor does he lie to him, nor does he hold him in contempt."

— A saying of Prophet Muḥammad ﷺ (Al-Nawawī's Forty Ḥadīth, No. 35)

This is how Muslims should be to each other—brothers and sisters who support one another and work together to live in a healthy Islamic society that is free from hatred or envy and full of peace and harmony for the sake of Allāh.

But what if your Muslim brother did something wrong or oppressed others?

Help him!

> Prophet Muḥammad ﷺ said: "Help your brother, whether he is an oppressor or he is oppressed."
>
> The people asked: "O Messenger of Allāh! We help the oppressed, but how do we help an oppressor?"
>
> The Prophet ﷺ said: "By seizing his hand [thereby preventing him from oppressing others]."
> *(Ṣaḥīḥ al-Bukhārī, No. 2444)*

Do Not Be Complacent

"Whoever amongst you sees an evil, he must change it with his hand; if he is unable to do so, then with his tongue; and if he is unable to do so, then with his heart; and that is the weakest form of faith."

— A saying of Prophet Muḥammad ﷺ (Riyāḍ al-Ṣāliḥīn, No. 184)

Whenever you see something that is displeasing to Allāh, do not hesitate to change it if you can.

Opportunities are all around us.

For example, you might remove some trash that is blocking the street or help kids in the neighborhood understand that it is wrong to tease animals. If you're a parent, you should also assess the children's books, toys, and games in your home to make sure they are appropriate for young Muslims. Make changes as needed.

Assess your own situation, too. If you are the owner of a business, for example, then you should take steps to make sure that all of your products and services are *ḥalāl*.[5]

Yet sometimes it's more complicated than that.

Maybe you work for others and do not own your own business. In that case, you might not have the freedom to change the things that are *ḥarām*.[6]

So, what can you do instead?

5. Permissible according to Islamic guidelines.
6. Prohibited according to Islamic guidelines.

Start by offering advice—and don't give up too quickly or easily. It may take some time to convince someone that a particular change is needed.

But what if your advice fails and you can't seem to find another job?

Keep trying, and be proactive about seeking out *ḥalāl* work. In the meantime, perhaps you could at least remove yourself from the *ḥarām* aspects of your job and perform another duty within the same company.

But what if this is not possible, and you are truly desperate for the work?

Then you should at least dislike this situation in your heart until you can do something about it. Ask Allāh ﷻ for His assistance, and continue doing whatever you can to distance yourself from the problem. Don't be complacent, and Allāh will bless your efforts, *in shā' Allāh*.

Complain to Allāh Alone

"And when the bearer of good tidings arrived, he cast it over his [Yaʿqūb's] face, and he returned [once again] seeing. He said, 'Did I not tell you that I know from Allāh that which you do not know?'"

— *Sūrat Yūsuf (Qur'ān 12:96)*

The story of Prophet Yaʿqūb (Jacob) (PBUH) teaches us a great lesson about patience.

Years passed, and he still didn't know anything about his son Yūsuf (Joseph) (PBUH), who had disappeared one day when his brothers secretly threw him into a well out of envy and jealousy.

Although they lied to their father and told him that Yūsuf (PBUH) was dead after being devoured by a wolf, he knew it wasn't true due to the weak evidence they showed him. In response to this, he said:

> "Rather, your souls have enticed you to something, so patience is most fitting. And Allāh is the one sought for help against that which you describe."
> — *Sūrat Yūsuf (Qur'ān 12:18)*

Yaʿqūb (PBUH) was so devastated when he lost another son of his that he actually became blind from grief,[7] yet he remained patient and trusted in Allāh.

His sons told him:

---

7. *Sūrat Yūsuf (Qur'ān 12:84)*

> "By Allāh, you will not cease remembering Yūsuf until you become fatally ill or become of those who perish."
> — *Sūrat Yūsuf (Qur'ān 12:85)*

To this, Ya'qūb (PBUH) responded:

> "I only complain of my suffering and my grief to Allāh, and I know from Allāh that which you do not know."
> — *Sūrat Yūsuf (Qur'ān 12:86)*

He also said:

> "Indeed, no one despairs of relief from Allāh except the disbelieving people."
> — *Sūrat Yūsuf (Qur'ān 12:87)*

Despite many long years of sadness and suffering, Ya'qūb (PBUH) never lost hope. Relief finally came when his sight was restored and he was reunited with his beloved sons.

Think about this story whenever you are facing hardship or struggle in your own life.

Long years may pass, and you may go through unbearable loss and pain—but if you are patient and trust in Allāh, He will not ever forget you or let you down.

Indeed, no one despairs of relief from Allāh except the disbelieving people!

It is going to get better, *in shā' Allāh.*

Have trust in Allāh's plans, be patient, and make *du'ā'*.

Be Kind to Children

"The Messenger of Allāh ﷺ came to some children who were playing and greeted them."

— Anas ibn Mālik (RA) (Sunan Abī Dā'ūd, No. 5202)

Prophet Muḥammad ﷺ was known for his good treatment of children.

He was kind to them, he played with them, and he gave them attention and respect.

Neither his age nor his status as a prophet made him act as though he was above greeting them.

Children are the hope for the future of society—and the way you treat them will always stay with them when they grow up.

Make an effort to make their childhoods positive and happy.

Do not look down on them or underestimate their intelligence and abilities.

Finally, remember that you are actually planting the seeds of their future morals and values inside of their hearts whenever you interact with them.

Forge Ahead and Do Not Give Up

"If people always give up whenever something is difficult, they will never succeed in either their worldly or religious affairs."

— *ʿUmar ibn ʿAbd al-ʿAzīz (Umayyad caliph, r. 717–720)*

Part of being tested in this worldly life has to do with your ability to endure the difficulties you face along the road.

Desirable results take time.

You can always take a break, but never stop.

Proceeding and forging ahead is what makes the difference.

May Allāh ﷻ ease the path for you and bless you in all of your endeavors.

Be Kind to the Elderly

"He who does not show mercy to our children or acknowledge the rights of our elderly is not one of us."

— A saying of Prophet Muḥammad ﷺ (Al-Adab al-Mufrad, No. 354)

Part of faith is being kind and respectful to the vulnerable segments of society.

Just as one should be kind to children, he also should respect the elderly and be gentle with them.

Sit with them, chat with them, listen to their stories, bring them gifts, and help them if they are in need as much as you can.

Allāh ﷻ will never forget the nice way you treated them.

Show People You Care

"It is also charity to utter a good word."

— A saying of Prophet Muḥammad ﷺ (Riyāḍ al-Ṣāliḥīn, No. 693)

It is well known that Islam places great emphasis on giving charity.

Charity helps people in need by alleviating some of their troubles. Why, then, is uttering a good word also regarded as a form of charity?

All human beings have problems and issues to deal with, including things that may worry or concern them.

That's why we should always try to make matters easier for one another rather than worse.

So, tell your loved ones how special they are to you. Focus on their good traits, and praise them for their positive qualities.

Thank people, check on them, tell them you care about them, and make sure they know that their existence matters.

Develop the Trait of Shyness

"Shyness brings nothing but good."

— A saying of Prophet Muḥammad ﷺ (Riyāḍ al-Ṣāliḥīn, No. 681)

The Islamic concept of shyness *(al-ḥayā')* has many layers to it. Among other things, people with this praiseworthy trait are shy of Allāh ﷻ before anyone else.

They weigh their words carefully before saying them. They are also modest and humble in the way they dress and interact with others.

They do not cross any red lines when it comes to their morals.

When you are truly shy of Allāh, this can only be good for you.

Allāh will be pleased with you, and you will be rewarded for your good character.

In addition, you will gain people's love and trust, and your conscience will be at peace.

Supplicate for Others

"I sought permission from the Prophet ﷺ to perform 'Umrah. He granted it to me and said, 'My brother, do not forget us in your supplications.' I would not exchange these words of his for the whole world."

— *'Umar ibn al-Khaṭṭāb (RA) (Riyāḍ al-Ṣāliḥīn, No. 713)*

Even the Prophet ﷺ asked his beloved Companions to make *du'ā'* for him.

Making *du'ā'* for one another is a great thing.

It purifies one's heart toward his or her Muslim brothers and sisters, spreading love and comfort between them.

The Prophet ﷺ said:

> "The supplication of a Muslim for his (Muslim) brother in his absence will certainly be answered. Every time he makes a supplication for good for his brother, the angel appointed for this particular task says: *Āmīn*! May it be for you, too."
> *(Riyāḍ al-Ṣāliḥīn, No. 1495)*

PERFECT YOUR WUḌŪ'

"When someone performs the wuḍū' perfectly [i.e., according to the sunnah of Prophet Muḥammad ﷺ], his sins depart from his body, even from under his nails."

— A saying of Prophet Muḥammad ﷺ (Riyāḍ al-Ṣāliḥīn, No. 1026)

The way you think about and perform *wuḍū'* (ablutions for prayer) won't ever be the same after you read this ḥadīth.

It is by the mercy of Allāh ﷻ that He provides us with so many varied ways to rid ourselves of sin.

The *wuḍū'* isn't just a means of physical purification; it also purifies the heart and soul.

Encourage your children and others who are still learning about prayer in Islam to perfect their *wuḍū'*. Tell them that it is their path to Jannah as it washes away all of their sins.

SEEK ALLĀH'S PROTECTION FROM EVIL

"[Were you not aware] that some verses were revealed [to me] tonight, the like of which has never been seen before? They are: {Say: I seek refuge in the Lord of daybreak}, and {Say: I seek refuge in the Lord of mankind}."

— A saying of Prophet Muḥammad ﷺ (Riyāḍ al-Ṣāliḥīn, No. 1014)

The best *du'ā's* one can recite to seek the protection of Allāh ﷻ are contained within the last two *sūrahs* (chapters) of the Qur'ān.

In the verses of *Sūrat al-Falaq* (Chapter 113), we ask Allāh ﷻ to protect us from different types of evil, including the dangers that come with darkness, the evil of those who practice witchcraft or magic, and the evils of the enviers when they practice their envy.

In *Sūrat al-Nās* (Chapter 114), we ask Allāh ﷻ to protect us from the whispers of those who make evil suggestions, whether they are of humankind or the jinn.

Note that Allāh ﷻ describes the devil's influence in the same *sūrah* as "retreating,"[8] meaning that it is weak and disappears as soon one remembers Allāh.

In other words, someone who relies on Allāh and keeps his or her tongue moist with the remembrance of Him will never be touched, hurt, or defeated by these types of evil.

The Prophet ﷺ advised his Muslim Companions to recite these two *sūrahs* twice a day, once in the morning upon waking up, and once in the evening before going to sleep.

8. Review Qur'ān 114:4.

PRAY TWO UNITS OF PRAYER BEFORE FAJR

"The Prophet ﷺ did not attach more importance to any nawāfil (supererogatory) prayer than he did to the two units of prayer before the dawn (fajr) prayer."

— ʿĀʾishah (RA) (Riyāḍ al-Ṣāliḥīn, No. 1101)

Simply praying two units of prayer before the obligatory Fajr Prayer is one of the best extra deeds one can do.

It is narrated that the Prophet ﷺ did not ever abandon this *sunnah* whether he was at home or traveling, which tells us how important and rewarding this prayer actually is.

Remain United

"And cooperate in righteousness and piety, but do not cooperate in sin and aggression."

— Sūrat al-Mā'idah (Qur'ān 5:2)

This verse from the Qur'ān talks about the Islamic concept of cooperation, which happens when a group of people gets together with the intention of spreading faith, harmony, justice, and other virtues that are of benefit to society.

This reminds me of the popular saying: "United we stand; divided we fall."

Unity is a key component in any plan to make positive changes in society, as a group will always be stronger than a single individual working on his or her own.

Islam makes it easy for Muslim communities to be unified, because it encourages people to come together in many different ways, whether it is for prayer and fasting in Ramaḍān, during prayer in general, in other Islamic rituals such as the Ḥajj pilgrimage, in its modest dress code for women, and so on and so forth.

To be unified, each individual should first start with himself, by making a conscious effort to choose the path that is most pleasing to Allāh ﷻ; then unity will spontaneously emerge after that.

Reconcile Between People

The Messenger of Allāh ﷺ said: "Shall I not tell you of what is better in rank than extra fasting, prayer, and charity?" They said: "Of course!" The Prophet ﷺ said: "Reconciliation between people."

— *Sunan al-Tirmidhī, No. 2509*

Reconciliation between people!

When you hear about a problem between your Muslim brothers or sisters, try your best to say good words that may help the situation.

Do not exploit it into an opportunity for gossip or feed into bad feelings.

When relations between people turn sour, this has a negative impact on society overall.

That's why we should always aim to play a positive role in any conflict and implant good feelings, thoughts, ideas, and energy among the people we care about.

Spread Peace and Harmony

"He who attempts to reconcile between people and speaks or conveys good [in order to avert a dispute] is not a liar."

— A saying of Prophet Muḥammad ﷺ (Al-Adab al-Mufrad, No. 385)

Let's say that two of your friends are no longer speaking together because of a minor disagreement they had. Is it okay to tell one of them that the other expressed a desire to reconcile, even if it is not technically true?

This is one of the few cases in which a Muslim may stretch the truth, but only because the aim is to bring about peace and harmony between others. Such words may generate positive feelings and help fix the issue between them.

In order not to lie, however, one may say carefully worded statements such as the following (altering names and other details as appropriate according to the specific circumstances): "When I spoke to Maryam the other day, I could see that she felt unhappy about what happened between the two of you. I think she probably really wants to work things out."

In addition, you should definitely not repeat anything bad that either of your friends said about the other. Emphasize the positive qualities found in each person, and continue to seek out creative ways to help restore the friendship.

Above all, remember the reason for your efforts, which is to spread peace and harmony rather than hatred, gossip, and slander. A Muslim should never partake in such activities, much less find enjoyment in them.

Have Faith in Allāh's Reward

"It was said, 'Enter Paradise.' He said, 'I wish my people could know of how my Lord has forgiven me and placed me among the honored.'"

— *Sūrat Yā-Sīn (Qur'ān 36:26–27)*

These verses are in the context of a story about a righteous man who advised the people of his land to follow the messengers sent by Allāh to deliver the message of *tawḥīd* (belief in One God), but the disbelievers did not like what he told them and arrogantly killed him.

When the man entered Paradise, he wished his people could know how happy and blessed he felt to be among the honored.

This verse is very soothing to the believers.

One should not worry too much about the worldly problems associated with this life.

It will all become a meaningless relic of the distant past once you are in Paradise, *in shā' Allāh.*

Do not despair, and do not allow your faith to weaken. Allāh ﷻ sees all of your efforts and will reward you greatly.

Work and Be Productive

"It is the reliant on Allāh who casts a grain under the earth and then relies on Allāh."

— *'Umar b. al-Khaṭṭāb (RA)*[9]

Relying on Allāh ﷻ does not mean that one should stop working so that he or she becomes in need of people. This is not reliance; it is dependence, which does not align with the purpose of human life, which includes being productive for the good of yourself, your family, your community, and society as a whole.

So, do your best to work and be productive. Never stop, yet rely on Allāh with every step you take.

That is how one benefits in both this worldly life and in the Hereafter.

9. As found in *The Compendium of Knowledge and Wisdom*, by Ibn Rajab (d. 1393).

FIND COMFORT IN ALLĀH'S PROMISE

"And they will say, 'Praise to Allāh, who has fulfilled for us His promise and made us inherit the earth [so] we may settle in Paradise wherever we will. And excellent is the reward of [righteous] workers.'"

— *Sūrat al-Zumar (Qur'ān 39:74)*

This is a beautiful verse that describes the state of the believers in the Hereafter.

They will feel both joy and gratitude upon recognizing that Allāh has fulfilled His promise to them and granted them Paradise.

Sometimes it may be difficult for us as human beings with limited knowledge of the unseen to imagine that this will really happen; this is why Allāh ﷻ comforts His servants in many verses of the Qur'ān, in order to remove any feelings of doubt or despair.

In a verse from *Sūrat Maryam*, for example, Allāh ﷻ tells us:

> "[Therein are] gardens of perpetual residence which the Most Merciful has promised His servants in the unseen. Indeed, His promise has ever been eminent."
> *(Qur'ān 19:61)*

In a verse from *Sūrat al-Rūm*, He also tells us:

> "Allāh does not fail in His promise, but most of the people do not know."
> *(Qur'ān 30:6)*

Never stop striving; never let yourself go astray.

Life is full of challenges, but Allāh's mercy encompasses all things, and will continue when you reach the eternal happiness found in Paradise, *in shā' Allāh*.

Don't Let Status Make You Arrogant

"When al-Fuḍayl b. ʿIyāḍ was asked about humbleness, he said: '[It is] submitting to the truth, yielding to it, and accepting it regardless of who utters it, even if the person is a young child or the most ignorant of people.'"

— Ibn al-Qayyim (Madārij al-Sālikīn)

You can always learn something new from every person you meet, so do not ever look down on someone just because he or she is younger or less knowledgeable.

If you are blessed with knowledge and status, this does not give you the right to mock people or disregard what they may say or suggest.

In many stories of the Companions (may Allāh ﷻ be pleased with them all), we see how they still listened to people and admitted to their mistakes, even after some of them had attained the status of caliph, which was the highest status one could attain as the leader of the Muslim *ummah*. Acknowledging the truth of a matter never made them feel any less, and their humble attitudes are what made them successful and beloved to their people.

No matter what status one may attain in life, we should always have the mentality that there is still room for improvement and much more to learn, keeping in mind that Allāh ﷻ may send us knowledge in unexpected ways.

It is also important to cultivate the ability to educate others through the knowledge Allāh has blessed us with, and this should ideally be done in the humblest way possible.

So, let the great principles found in Islam be your guide as you continue to receive (and transmit) knowledge.

Refrain from Excessive Eating and Talking

"There are two habits that harden the heart: too much talking and too much eating."

— Al-Fuḍayl b. ʿIyāḍ (d. 803)

Islam teaches us to be moderate in everything we do.

Talking more than needed can definitely lead one to make mistakes and misjudge the appropriateness of certain topics, while excessive eating results in laziness and leads one to follow the path of desires. Left uncontrolled, both of these things may damage our faith.

If you are interested in the topic of eating as it relates to faith, I would advise you to read the eleventh chapter of *The Revival of the Religious Sciences (On the Manners Related to Eating)*, by Imām Abū Ḥāmid al-Ghazālī (d. 1111).

Islam helps us exercise moderation in our speech by emphasizing that one should either say good words or simply remain silent, which is something one will be rewarded for by Allāh.

Moderation in the way we eat is built through fasting.

Other than the obligatory month of fasting that takes place in Ramaḍān, Muslims are encouraged to fast on many other days as well.

Fasting on the Day of ʿArafāt, for example, expiates the sins of the past year and the one after.

In addition, remember the words of Prophet Muḥammad ﷺ, who said:

> "A human being cannot fill a vessel worse than his stomach. A few morsels that keep his back upright are sufficient for him. If he must, then he should keep one third for food, one third for drink, and one third for his breathing."
> *(Riyāḍ al-Ṣāliḥīn, No. 515)*

Make it a Habit to Smile

"I have not seen anyone who smiled more than the Messenger of Allāh ﷺ."

— 'Abd Allāh ibn al-Ḥārith (RA) (Jāmi' al-Tirmidhī, No. 3641)

One can only imagine how much work, stress, and pressure Prophet Muḥammad ﷺ had while fulfilling his duties as a prophet.

He literally built a whole new nation from scratch with the help of Allāh's guidance.

The weight of the world was on his shoulders, and he also had to deal with different types of people, some of whom weren't very nice.

Yet he never used this as an excuse to display a bad temper.

To the contrary, he was known amongst his people for his smiling face!

Smiling spreads positivity and lessens unwelcome feelings of stress and tension, relaxing both your muscles and your soul.

Whatever you are doing right now, take a deep breath and smile!

There is nothing in this world that is worth the loss of your smile; in fact, your smile may actually make any burdens you are carrying much easier to bear.

Stop the Sins of Backbiting and Gossiping

"And do not spy or backbite each other. Would one of you like to eat the flesh of his brother when dead? You would detest it. And fear Allāh; indeed, Allāh is Accepting of Repentance and Merciful."

— Sūrat al-Ḥujurāt (Qur'ān 49:12)

In the above verse of the Qur'ān, Allāh ﷻ describes the act of backbiting as eating the flesh of your dead brother, showing how vile this behavior truly is.

Yet many casually engage in backbiting and gossiping without fully understanding the serious nature of these sins.

If you find yourself falling into this type of idle talk, make a pledge to stop.

Once you succeed at breaking this habit, the quality of your life will become much better.

It is literally like losing extra weight that creates a burden on your soul!

If you feel the urge to talk about someone behind his or her back, remember these lines of poetry authored by Imām al-Shāfi'ī:

> "Do not allow your tongue to mention another person's faults.
> You, too, are full of faults, and others have tongues as well."

With the right intention, you will succeed at breaking this habit, *in shā' Allāh.*

No matter what you may have said about someone in the past, ask Allāh for forgiveness, and try your best to mention the person's good qualities to others whenever possible.

In addition, the great scholar al-Ḥasan al-Baṣrī (d. 728) said that the atonement for backbiting is to ask for forgiveness for the person you wronged through your backbiting.

Study Islam, Not Muslims

"Obey me so long as I obey Allāh and His Messenger; if I disobey Allāh and His Messenger, you must not obey me."

— *Abū Bakr al-Ṣiddīq (RA)*[10]

These words were said by Abū Bakr al-Ṣiddīq (RA) when he was chosen to lead the Muslim *ummah* (nation) as caliph after the death of Prophet Muḥammad ﷺ. In the same speech, he also said: "If I do good, help me, and if I do wrong, correct me."

Abū Bakr's wise approach to leadership teaches us an important lesson.

People will always have flaws and shortcomings no matter how great their status (or how knowledgeable they are)—and this is precisely why we should never blindly follow another human being when it comes to learning about our religion.

Also, one should not judge Islam strictly by the actions of its adherents.

Ideally, you should be able to do so—and most Muslims are undoubtedly sincere in their practice of Islam. Unfortunately, however, not everyone who calls himself a Muslim is a real Muslim, and not everyone who appears to be religious is actually knowledgeable about the religion. In addition, one may be sincere but unknowingly convey incorrect information to others.

10. As recorded by Ibn Kathīr in *al-Bidāyah wa-al-Nihāyah.*

In short, people make mistakes, but Allāh never does. Follow the advice of knowledgeable and trustworthy people so long as they are also following Allāh's path. We are blessed to know what Allāh wants of us in the Qur'ān—so read His perfect words, and you will never be misled, *in shā' Allāh.*

Maintain Healthy Boundaries

"And behave decently toward people."

— A saying of Prophet Muḥammad ﷺ (Riyāḍ al-Ṣāliḥīn, No. 61)

This ḥadīth teaches us to maintain our manners when dealing with people no matter who they are. Yet treating people nicely and being humble with them as required in Islam does not mean that we should not maintain healthy boundaries as well.

One can be firm but still remain kind and decent for the sake of Allāh.

Adopting this strategy helps preserve a sense of respect in our relationships. For example, friends, and even spouses, should still be polite with each other and choose their words carefully when discussing sensitive topics.

Using a bit of wisdom in the way we handle our relationships is a good habit that also teaches our children to have healthy boundaries, and thus decency, in their relationships in the future as well.

Be Kind to Your Family

"I served Allāh's Messenger ﷺ for ten years, and he never said 'Uff!' to me. He never asked me about something I had done, saying, 'Why did you do that?' Nor [did he ever ask me] about something I had left undone, saying, 'Why did you leave it undone?'"

— Anas ibn Mālik (RA) (Al-Shamā'il al-Muḥammadiyyah, No. 344)

If this was the way Prophet Muḥammad ﷺ treated his servant, what about the way we treat our sons, daughters, and spouses?

Being a parent or the head of a household does not give one the authority to tyrannize those living in his or her home.

Home is supposed to be a place of comfort for everyone.

Be gentle, even when someone makes a mistake. There is almost always a kinder way to deliver the message.

Remember the words of Prophet Muḥammad ﷺ, who told his wife 'Ā'ishah (RA):

> "O 'Ā'ishah! Be kind, for if Allāh wants good for the people of a household, he will bring kindness to them.
> *(Ṣaḥīḥ al-Targhīb wa-al-Tarhīb, No. 2669)*

Find True Love

"When one acts upon the obedience of Allāh, Allāh will love him, and if Allāh loves him, He will make him beloved to His people."

— *Abū al-Dardā' al-Anṣārī (RA)*[11]

Finding love and acceptance among the people whom you meet from day to day is a clear blessing and a sign from Allāh ﷻ showing that He loves you, and that you are on the right path.

But does this mean that you won't ever have haters? Absolutely not.

Sadly, not all people are spiritually healthy; as such, they are not in a position to recognize or appreciate the goodness found in others. However, the meaning of the above quote is that the other good people of this world will recognize you when they find you, and they will often be of help and comfort to you in this life, making *du'ā'* for you and supporting you in other ways.

This is an example of true love, showing how Allāh ﷻ rewards and blesses His faithful servants in this worldly life.

11. As recorded by Aḥmad ibn Ḥanbal in *al-Zuhd.*

Spread Greetings of Peace

"By Him in Whose Hand is my life! You will not enter Jannah until you believe, and you will not believe until you love one another. Shall I inform you of something which, if you do, you will love one another? Spread salām [greetings of peace] amongst yourselves."

— A saying of Prophet Muḥammad ﷺ (Riyāḍ al-Ṣāliḥīn, No. 847)

Try it! Whenever you encounter a friend or meet someone for the first time, or even when you pass a stranger on the street or enter someone's home or another building, say "al-salāmu ʿalaykum" (peace be upon you).

Don't sit and wonder why the other person didn't greet you first; this is unproductive! Break the ice by spreading greetings of peace, and you will notice how this act alone creates an atmosphere of love and positivity.

Cultivate Patience

"We found that the best days of our lives were due to patience."

— *'Umar ibn al-Khaṭṭāb (RA)*[12]

This is a great inspirational statement indicating that patience grants one the best quality of life.

This is because patience requires a combination of strength, faith, discipline, and gratitude, which are some of the best attributes one can have.

Patience is one of the main concepts we learn when fasting the month of Ramaḍān, and this is one reason why fasting is greatly rewarded by Allāh ﷻ.

As narrated by a Companion of Prophet Muḥammad ﷺ named Sahl (RA):

> "In Paradise, there is a gate called al-Rayyān. On the Day of Resurrection, it will be said: 'Where are those who used to fast? Would you like to enter through al-Rayyān? Whoever enters through it will never thirst again.' Then when they have entered, [the gate] will be closed behind them, and no one but they will enter through it."
> *(Sunan al-Nasā'ī, No. 2237)*

It is thus no coincidence that Imām Ḥasan al-Baṣrī (d. 728) called patience "one of the treasures of Paradise."

12. As recorded by Aḥmad ibn Ḥanbal in *al-Zuhd*.

Work Hard to Enter Paradise

Abū Bakr (RA) asked, "Will anybody be called from all of those gates?" [Prophet Muḥammad ﷺ] replied, "Yes, and I hope that you will be one of them."

— *Riyāḍ al-Ṣāliḥīn, No. 1216*

This quote comes in the context of a ḥadīth in which Prophet Muḥammad ﷺ informed his Companions (may Allāh ﷻ be pleased with them all) about the gates of Jannah. He said that the believer would be called from the gate associated with whichever good deed he had engaged in during this worldly life. For example, someone who performed extra prayers would be called from the Gate of Prayer, while someone who gave extra charity would be called from the Gate of Charity.

This prompted Abū Bakr (RA) to ask if one could be granted the blessing of being called from all of these gates, and the response of the Prophet ﷺ was to say yes.

Work hard to enter all of the gates of Paradise, where you will be a companion of the Prophet ﷺ and his beloved Companions, *in shā' Allāh!*

Have Positive Expectations of the Creator

Anas ibn Mālik (RA) reported: "The Prophet ﷺ entered the home of a young man in the throes of death. The Prophet ﷺ said, 'How do you feel?' The man said, 'By Allāh, O Messenger of Allāh, I hope in Allāh, and I am fearful regarding my sins.' The Prophet ﷺ said, 'These two feelings are not combined in the heart of a servant in such circumstances but that Allāh will grant him what he hopes and make him safe from what he fears.'"

— *Jāmiʿ al-Tirmidhī, No. 983*

The sentiments expressed by this man while on his death-bed are closely related to the concept of *ḥusn al-ẓann billāh*, which means having a positive outlook toward Allāh ﷻ (or good expectations of the Creator).

As a believer, you have trust in Allāh and hope that He will reward you for any good that you have done throughout your life, yet you remain fearful regarding the sins you committed, because you know that you could have definitely made better choices while you still had the chance.

We can see how merciful Allāh is from the response of the Prophet ﷺ. If you feel the same way this man did, Allāh will grant you what you hope and make you safe from what you fear.

The above shows us that having a positive outlook toward Allāh ﷻ requires one to be sincere; it is not enough to think that Allāh will reward you if you have no regrets over your sins. In addition, one must also work to refrain from sins and repent from any mistakes as they occur.

Being sincere about your good expectations of the Creator also means (by Allāh's will) that you will be granted blessings that are far beyond anything you ever expected. So, do not delay your repentance. Show remorse for your sins and rectify your shortcomings now rather than while you are in the throes of death—and always trust in Allāh and ask Him to grant you the best.

The Messenger of Allāh ﷺ said:

> "Allāh the Exalted says: 'I am as my slave expects me to be, and I am with him when he remembers Me. If he remembers Me inwardly, I will remember him inwardly, and if he remembers Me in an assembly, I will remember him in a better assembly [i.e., in the assembly of angels].'"
> *(Riyāḍ al-Ṣāliḥīn, No. 1435)*

Seek Knowledge for His Sake

"Whenever she heard anything which she did not understand, she used to ask again till she understood it completely."

— *Ibn Abī Mulaykah (Ṣaḥīḥ al-Bukhārī, No. 103)*

The above statement was made in reference to the Prophet's wife ʿĀʾishah (RA), showing the great value she placed on knowledge and accuracy.

Islam does not tell us to blindly follow without understanding; it actually gives us the tools to help our minds expand.

As such, do not ever shun or avoid beneficial knowledge. The knowledge we gain throughout our lives helps make us better Muslims and leads to improvements in our communities when we act upon what we learn.

This is what the wives and noble Companions of the Prophet ﷺ (may Allāh be pleased with them all) taught us by asking questions and openly discussing various matters pertaining to religion and everyday life. They sought true understanding and transferred their knowledge to others. As knowledge spread, scholarship thrived under Islam for many generations (continuing until the present day), also giving rise to a "Golden Age" of science and technology that lasted for hundreds of years.

In our time period, we are blessed with the ability to obtain information almost instantly. But with this blessing comes great responsibilities as well.

Not all information is worth acquiring—so always remember to use sound judgment when browsing the many websites, books, lectures, and other resources available to us. This means taking care to seek out authentic sources of knowledge, but it also means thinking critically and reading widely in order to gain a diverse range of perspectives. In addition, we should always remember to use our minds and avoid glorifying another person's words or opinions. Be sincere, and seek knowledge with the right intentions.

As Allāh ﷻ informs us in *Sūrat al-Nūr*: "Allāh is the Light of the heavens and the earth," and He "guides to His light whom He wills." *(Qur'ān 24:35)*

Understand that the path to enlightenment is illuminated by Allāh through His guidance, so always strive to be among those who seek knowledge for His sake.

> "Allāh will raise those who have believed among you and those who were given knowledge, by degrees. And Allāh is Aware of what you do."
> *— Sūrat al-Mujādalah (Qur'ān 58:11)*

Safeguard Yourself Against Materialism

"Do not extend your eyes toward that by which We have given enjoyment to [certain] categories of them [i.e., the disbelievers], and do not grieve over them."

— Sūrat al-Ḥijr (Qur'ān 15:88)

Yes, sometimes the people who go astray seem to be more privileged in this worldly life from a materialistic perspective.

In this verse of the Qur'ān, Allāh ﷻ is telling Prophet Muḥammad ﷺ not to grieve over any prosperity enjoyed by the disbelievers.

He also reminds the Prophet ﷺ that he has been provided with something much better:

> "And We have certainly given you, [O Muḥammad], seven of the often repeated [verses] [Sūrah al-Fātiḥah] and the great Qur'ān."
> *— Sūrat al-Ḥijr (Qur'ān 15:87)*

My dear believer, the Qur'ān is what helps one maintain his or her faith, and it is this faith that will always remind you that our permanent abode is the life of the Hereafter.

In His infinite mercy, Allāh ﷻ has provided all of us with the guidance and tools we need to follow the path of truth—yet some people deliberately take a different path.

So, do not grieve over those who are misguided and drowning in materialism, as such people will not understand where true satisfaction lies until they deliberately choose faith and leave the other stuff behind.

But what about a believer who falls into the trap of giving undue priority to wealth, fame, looks, and popularity above all else?

Again, faith is the answer, as this will help one quickly realize that the choice to abandon corruption is a superior choice that is much better for the soul. But faith must be cultivated over time, and this is why we must always stay connected to the Qurʾān (and our prayers), surround ourselves with good people, and make *duʿāʾ* not to fall into materialism and other unhealthy behaviors.

CHECK ON PEOPLE

"And to walk with a Muslim brother of mine to meet his needs is dearer to me than observing i'tikāf[13] in this mosque (meaning the mosque of Madīnah) for a month."

— *A saying of Prophet Muḥammad ﷺ (Al-Targhīb wa-al-Tarhīb, No. 2623)*

People who think that Islam is only about praying and fasting should re-evaluate their understanding of the religion.

Allāh ﷻ has required these rituals of us so that we may become better people who make a difference in the world by helping others. If these acts of worship do not have that effect on us, then we need to work on strengthening our faith.

As narrated in the same ḥadīth cited above, the Prophet ﷺ also said:

> "The most beloved of people to Allāh is the one who brings most benefit to people, and the most beloved of deeds to Allāh, may He be exalted, is bringing joy to a Muslim, or relieving him of hardship, or paying off his debt, or warding off hunger from him."

So, remember to check on the people you know, including your family members, your friends, your neighbors, and your Muslim brothers and sisters in faith. If you are doing well, don't assume that everyone else is doing well. Always offer a helping hand whenever you can, whether it is to provide knowledge, counseling, financial assistance, or another service that can help someone who needs it. If this is not possible, then at least

13. To take up residence in the mosque for a period of time for the sole purpose of worship.

visit or check up on your loved ones with a call or a message. The Prophet ﷺ ended the ḥadīth with the following words:

> "[When] someone walks with his Muslim brother to meet his need, Allāh will make him stand firm on the Day when all feet will slip [The Day of Judgment]."

Cleanse the Heart

"The remedy for the heart is five things: reciting the Qur'ān and pondering over its meaning, keeping the stomach empty,[14] standing for prayer at night, humbly supplicating to Allāh in the early morning hours before dawn, and sitting with the righteous."

— Ibrāhīm al-Khawwāṣ (d. 904)

The five things mentioned in this quote cure a Muslim's heart from worries, hatred, envy, and a plethora of other ailments that may affect his or her relations with others.

They provide one with a sense of peace and ease and work to increase faith and good morals.

As we have already spoken in detail about some of these topics throughout this book, we shall next focus on just two items from this list: standing for prayer at night and humbly supplicating to Allāh in the early morning hours before dawn.

14. Keeping the stomach empty means to refrain from overeating and may also imply the practice of fasting.

Supplicate Just Before Dawn

"I am the Lord; I am the Lord! Who is there to supplicate to Me so that I may respond to him? Who is there to ask Me a favor so that I may grant it to him? Who is there to ask for forgiveness from Me so that I may forgive him?"

— Ṣaḥīḥ Muslim, No. 758b

As narrated in the above-cited ḥadīth, Prophet Muḥammad ﷺ informed his Companions that Allāh ﷻ "descends every night to the lowest heaven when one-third of the first part of the night is over" and says the above words, "continuing like this until the day breaks."

This ḥadīth draws attention to the unique blessings that can be found each night in the time period just before dawn. While most people are fast asleep in bed, there are a few very special people who wake up at that hour and deny themselves the comfort that sleep brings and the innate desire of every human being to rest.

Waking up for the fajr (dawn) prayer required of all Muslims is already very challenging for many people, so what can we say about those who wake up before dawn merely for the sake of becoming closer to Allāh ﷻ? This is why Allāh mentioned them in the Qur'ān as being among the privileged:

> "Indeed, the righteous will be among gardens and springs, accepting what their Lord has given them. Indeed, they were before that doers of good. They used to sleep but little of the night, and in the hours before dawn they would ask forgiveness."
> *— Sūrat al-Dhāriyāt (Qur'ān 51:15–18)*

GAIN THE BLESSINGS OF QIYĀM AL-LAYL

"Do not give up Qiyām al-Layl (praying at night), for the Messenger of Allāh ﷺ never abandoned it. Whenever he fell ill or became lethargic, he would pray while sitting."

— 'Ā'ishah (RA) (Sunan Abī Dā'ūd, No. 1307)

Although Qiyām al-Layl refers to optional night prayers that are not among the five daily prayers required of a Muslim, the Prophet ﷺ never abandoned it, which tells us how important it is.

In a verse from *Sūrat al-Zumar*, Allāh ﷻ says:

> "Is one who is devoutly obedient during periods of the night, prostrating and standing [in prayer], fearing the Hereafter and hoping for the mercy of his Lord, [like one who does not]? Say, 'Are those who know equal to those who do not know?' Only they will remember [who are] people of understanding."
> *(Qur'ān 39:9)*

Qiyām al-Layl brings one closer to Allāh ﷻ and may be a reason for your sins to be forgiven and your supplications answered.

But what if someone could not pray Qiyām al-Layl due to his or her work schedule or other circumstances that make it difficult to pray at night? Will such a person lose the blessings associated with these prayers?

Ibn 'Abbās (RA) said that someone who prays the 'Ishā' prayer in congregation with the firm (sincere) intention to also pray Fajr in congregation has fulfilled the requirements of Qiyām al-Layl.[15]

15. Based on the words of the Prophet ﷺ, as recorded in *Sunan Abī Dā'ūd (No. 555)* and elsewhere.

The Prophet ﷺ also said:

> "Anyone who regularly offers prayer at night but (on a certain night) is dominated by sleep will be given the reward of praying. His sleep will be almsgiving [from Allāh to the person, because He rewarded him for his sleep as if he had prayed]."
> *(Sunan Abī Dā'ūd, No. 1314)*

Make Excuses for People

"If you hear something that you dislike about your brother, try your best to find an excuse for him, and if you did not find an excuse for him, tell yourself that perhaps my brother has an excuse that I am not aware of."

— Abū Qilābah (d. 722)

Never make a hasty judgment about your Muslim brother or sister because of something you heard from a third party. Even when you believe you have direct knowledge of something, it may be that you do not actually have the full story or correctly understand the person's intentions.

People's hearts are sometimes full of painful secrets, which can be difficult to understand when you are not going through the same trials in life. What's more, people have different ways of coping with their problems, and this is one reason why we should try our best to assume good of them even when their actions don't immediately make sense to us.

For example, maybe someone you know extremely well did not bring you a gift on a special occasion when gifts are the norm in your culture and you have always exchanged gifts in the past. Or maybe a good friend has stopped responding to your invitations or making any effort to visit you. Maybe he or she no longer seems to answer your messages or phone calls in the first place. Even worse, maybe someone has told you that your friend said something bad about you behind your back!

Despite everything, do not rush to cut ties with this person or end the friendship you have enjoyed together. It may be that your friend is going through a major hardship at the moment that you know nothing about!

What if, for example, your friend (or a close relative of your friend) has an illness that they prefer not to reveal or talk about? Or what if the person who gossiped about them to you actually told you a lie that your friend is not even aware of? There are many possibilities to consider, all of them equally valid. For example, maybe your friend does not visit or bring gifts because they are short on cash and feel embarrassed about this.

Yes, it feels extremely hurtful when someone seems to be ignoring you for no reason at all, but so long as the person has not directly displayed any bad intentions toward you, you should always try to give them the benefit of the doubt and assume that they mean no harm, just like you may someday be in need of other people's understanding and hope for them to make excuses for you as well. So, remain polite—and try talking to your friend!

Also remember what Allāh ﷻ has told us in a verse of *Sūrat al-Ḥujurāt:*

> "O you who have believed, avoid suspicion as much (as possible). Indeed, some suspicion is a sin. And do not spy or backbite each other. Would one of you like to eat the flesh of his brother when dead? You would detest it. And fear Allāh; indeed, Allāh is Accepting of Repentance and Merciful."
> *(Qur'ān 49:12)*

A Final Word: Keep Striving

"No one ever wrote a book without one day [in the future] saying, 'Had such-and-such been changed, it would have been better; had such-and-such been added, it would have been more acceptable; had such-and-such been stated earlier, it would have been preferable; and had such-and-such been omitted, it would have been more elegant.' Such a phenomenon is one of the great lessons and evidence of the imperfection [found in] all human beings."

— Al-Qāḍī al-Fāḍil ʿAbd al-Raḥīm al-Bīsānī ("The Excellent Judge") (d. 1199)

With this quote, dear reader, I end this book, which I hope had a positive impact on you. If my writing succeeded in helping you learn more about the blessed religion of Islam or encouraged you to become a better Muslim, it is only by the will of Allāh ﷻ—while if I neglected anything within these pages or made a mistake of any kind, it is due to my own ignorance and shortcomings.

As for the book's impact on my own soul, I can tell you that the person who finished writing this book (all thanks to Allāh) is not the same person who sat down to write it, yet it is to be expected that I may one day in the future wish that I had written it differently (and better) as Allāh ﷻ guides me according to His will to acquire more knowledge throughout my life.

And so it is with every experience we go through in our lives; we must learn from it, whether voluntarily or involuntarily—because this is how Allāh ﷻ created us as human beings, with a great capacity for learning and improving as we reach new understanding and ultimately change for the better. This is actually why I love change! While many people view change as something negative to be avoided, change that is purely for the sake of Allāh ﷻ signals growth and cannot be anything but positive.

Life is beautiful, so go out and experience new things. So long as you always take care to stay within the limits ordained to us by Allāh, the new things you learn in this life will only expand your mind and make you a better person.

Every single one of us has imperfections and shortcomings that need to be improved, but this should not leave us paralyzed or make us feel that we are unable to make positive contributions to the world we live in. Whatever we do in life, we should try our best according to the level of knowledge and experience we possess at the time—yet it is also very normal to later recognize that there were things we could have done much better.

So, do not blame yourself for this universal phenomenon that all humans experience, and simply recognize that this is the way Allāh ﷻ created us—to find the path that is most pleasing to Him for the benefit of ourselves and others during our short time in this worldly life.

In a verse from *Sūrat al-Baqarah*, Allāh ﷻ tells us the following:

> "Allāh does not charge a soul except [with that within] its capacity. It will have [the consequence of] what [good] it has gained, and it will bear [the consequence of] what [evil] it has earned."
> *(Qur'ān 2:286)*

This is a reminder that Allāh ﷻ does not make us bear what we cannot, providing us with the motivation to always strive harder no matter what challenges we may face in life.

The conclusion of this verse contains a supplication that a believer should make to Allāh in recognition of his or her flaws, and to ask the Creator for forgiveness, guidance, and mercy:

> "Our Lord! Do not impose blame upon us if we have forgotten or erred. Our Lord! Lay not upon us a burden like that which You laid upon those before us. Our Lord! Burden us not with that which we have no ability to bear. And pardon us; and forgive us; and have mercy upon us. You are our protector, so give us victory over the disbelieving people."

Manufactured by Amazon.ca
Acheson, AB

10313554R00085